Praise for *How To Build The Dental Practice of Your Dreams (Without Killing Yourself!) in Less Than 60 Days*

"For decades now, I have recommended Michael Gerber's E-Myth Revisited as the go-to entrepreneurial guide. After reading David Moffet's *How To Build The Dental Practice of Your Dreams (Without Killing Yourself!) in Less Than 60 Days,* I now say that same thing to any and all dentists. David Moffet walks his talk and has not only built a thriving and successful dental practice but a life of wonder and enrichment as well. Anyone aspiring to build both a thriving dental practice and life, READ this book. It has all the secrets to such success!"

—Jack Daly

CEO JackDaly.net

"This book not only teaches how to create the ultimate patient experience, it is a game plan on how to become a business customers cannot live without. Moffet did exactly that and now shares how you can too. Everyone in your organization needs to read this book."

—John R. DiJulius III

Author of The Customer Service Revolution

"David has a natural passion for patient awareness and service. This passion and talent is what every professional needs to be able to survive in today's highly competitive market. As science-trained human beings, for many it's not a natural talent. This book outlines the understanding of why you need to focus on world-class service to fast track the success of your profession. The book will inspire you, motivate you, and keep you loving the world of dentistry, not dreading it."

—Kathy Metaxas

Director, Consultant, International Speaker, and Professional Motivator

"David Moffet is a foremost leader in the field of dental practice building. His book How to Build the Dental Practice of Your Dreams (Without Killing Yourself!) in Less Than 60 Days is a must-have for any dentist who wants to enjoy the lifestyle we were promised in dental school. David provides proven, hands-on practical advice to avoid what he calls drudgery dentistry. Every dentist has the power to maximize profit and run his practice on his own terms. Want to work three days a week instead of five? Want to raise your fees without losing any patients? Read this book!"

—Dr. David M. Madow

Cofounder, The Madow Group

"Jim Rohn said that, 'we could all use a little coaching. When you're playing the game, it's hard to think of everything.' In this book Dr. Moffet teaches us that a dental practice passionately devoted to extraordinary service will have only one worry about profits: They will be embarrassingly large! He encourages his readers to let no one ever come to you without leaving better and happier. David's premise is simple: the secret to success is not a secret…work hard, shift your thinking, and add real value to people's lives."

—Ronald F. Arndt, *DDS, MBA, MAGD*

Master & Board Certified Coach
THE DENTAL COACH

"Don't just read this book. Use this book. Dr. Moffet provides you the playbook for the Ultimate Dentists' Experience, revealing how to build a successful seven-figure practice while working four days a week for 37 weeks."

—Shep Hyken

Customer Service Expert and New York Times *bestselling*
Author of The Amazement Revolution

"David Moffet is not only a world class dentist but a world class author and consultant. As David says in his book, 'It is easy to have phenomenal growth in one's practice when the patient is your first priority.' In the chapters of his book he will give you dozens of put-to-use-tomorrow ideas of getting the results you desire in referrals from existing patients as well as revenue enhancement. He is a pro at getting the team engaged in helping their dentist create this world-class environment. The best dentists and practices always want to be better. David Moffet can give you the tools to continue building your dream practice year after year while enjoying more freedom to enjoy your other life."

—Linda Miles

Founder, Linda Miles & Associates
Founder, Speaking Consulting Network
Cofounder, Oral Cancer Cause (a 5013c)

"*How to Build the Dental Practice of Your Dreams (Without Killing Yourself!) in Less Than 60 Days* is a practical guide based on decades of experience. Dr. David Moffet gives wise advice that can help readers be better business people and better clinicians. When dentists have their practice under control they can focus more on patients, and Dr. Moffet's advice will help readers strike this balance. His advice is clear, accessible, and applicable, and the book is fun to read. Whether you're just starting your practice or you're looking for that next stage of growth, this book will help."

—Dr. Howard Farran, MBA

International Lecturer and Publisher/Founder of Dentaltown Magazine

HOW TO BUILD THE DENTAL PRACTICE OF YOUR DREAMS

(WITHOUT KILLING YOURSELF!)

IN LESS THAN 60 DAYS

HOW TO BUILD THE DENTAL PRACTICE OF YOUR DREAMS (WITHOUT KILLING YOURSELF!) IN LESS THAN 60 DAYS

DR. DAVID MOFFET

THE #1 AUTHORITY IN WORLD CLASS DENTAL CUSTOMER SERVICE

Published by Advantage, Charleston, South Carolina.
Member of Advantage Media Group.

ADVANTAGE is a registered trademark and the Advantage colophon is a trademark of Advantage Media Group, Inc.

Printed in the United States of America.

ISBN: 978-1-59932-521-7
LCCN: 2015935948

Advantage Media Group is proud to be a part of the Tree Neutral® program. Tree Neutral offsets the number of trees consumed in the production and printing of this book by taking proactive steps such as planting trees in direct proportion to the number of trees used to print books. To learn more about Tree Neutral, please visit **www.treeneutral.com**. To learn more about Advantage's commitment to being a responsible steward of the environment, please visit **www.advantagefamily.com/green**

Advantage Media Group is a publisher of business, self-improvement, and professional development books and online learning. We help entrepreneurs, business leaders, and professionals share their Stories, Passion, and Knowledge to help others Learn & Grow. Do you have a manuscript or book idea that you would like us to consider for publishing? Please visit **advantagefamily.com** or call **1.866.775.1696.**

To my parents, Rod and Jean, who taught me what's right and what's wrong, and who instilled in me those values to enable me to know the difference…

And to my wife Jayne, and our three children, James, Kate and Thomas, who've each had a significant impact on making this journey such an interesting and worthwhile expedition, so far…

ACKNOWLEDGEMENTS

Building the Dental Practice of your Dreams is an impossible task, if you try to do it on your own.

That's a given.

The Dental Practice that I built in the heart of Western Sydney, in the working class heart of Sydney, would not have been possible at all without the help and contributions from the following people:

Firstly, my wonderfully loyal patients. To those people who chose to put their unconditional trust in me for their dental health, I thank you dearly. My Dental Practice would have been nothing without you. It was because of this trust that I strove every day, to make each of your visits to the dentist as memorable as they could be. In a nice, pleasant sort of way. Not the traditional way that the public views Dentistry.

To my advisors, throughout my career in Dentistry, I offer my heartfelt thanks. Each one of you has made a contribution that has molded me into the person I have become, and each of you has added influence into the Practice that I created. To Jon Kozeniauskas and Erika King, I say thank you, for setting me onto the path of Dental Improvement, and for showing me, that anything is possible. Giles Patterson, as a non-dental coach in business, I've never worked so hard as the twelve months I worked with you, and boy, was it worth it! Carol Davis, Philip Palmer, Michael Sernik; thank you all for your impacts on my practice and the direction it took.

To my Dental Mentors, I owe great thanks. Firstly Linda Miles. The doyenne of modern dental management. Thank you for your words of encouragement and for always being available for advice and support. And Dr Ron Arndt, my late in life Dental Friend, you are an inspiration. Thank you so much for your assistance, friendship, and wisdom.

Kathy Metaxis, David Madow, Richard Madow. Thank you. As popular dental speakers and presenters, you've shown me the way.

And Ed O'Keeffe. Your mastermind meetings were just what the Doctor ordered, and at the right time in my life. They expanded and broadened my thinking in an exponential manner. If it wasn't for you Ed, I'd have never known that there was a whole big world of wonderful dental people out there across the pond. You know them. Mark, Karen, Harry, Scott, Rob. It's a big list…

Also Ed, you introduced me to John DiJulius, who provided the "glue" for putting my pieces together. John, your encouragement, your friendship, your support, was what brought it all together. I knew what I did, I just didn't know what I did. John, you helped turn the intangible into the tangible. Thank you.

Jack Daly. Thanks for the push, in the right direction, to get this book on its way. It won't be an only child. Jack, you're an inspiration. I wish I had half your energy! It's an honour to be your friend.

Craig Garber. Thanks. You know what you've done.

Back home, I guess I'd have never made this giant leapfrog without the encouragements I received and the friendships that I made in the Exceptional Practice Group of Dentists. To our moderator, Winston Marsh CSP, your encouragement and words of wisdom have made a distinct impression upon the point in my life that I stand at today. To Mark, Jamie, Harry, Wally, Phil; thank you too for your regular inputs and encouragements.

To George Lee, I guess my best Dental buddy, thanks for sharing the Dental and Non-Dental journeys of the last twenty-two years. George, with you, we discovered the knowledges and wisdoms of Zig Ziglar, Jim Rohn, Tom Hopkins, and Dan Kennedy. I can say it is great to have sat in the audiences of all these great men. They all had influence upon the place that I've arrived at today…

Finally, and most importantly, I owe my deepest thanks to my long term business partner, wife and best friend, Jayne Bandy, for her unconditional faith and belief in me, and her trust, that right is right. Jayne, none of what I have achieved could have been achieved without you. It is said, that behind every great man stands a great woman. Well, in your case Jayne, it's an honour to have you standing right there beside me.

TABLE OF CONTENTS

INTRODUCTION

THE JOURNEY TO SUCCESS

According to Dr. Omer Reed, a startling ninety-five percent of US dentists are still drilling teeth at age sixty-five, an age when most other Americans are getting ready to retire. But these "drillers" won't have the luxury of retiring. Despite a lifetime of hard work, they'll still be tied to their dental chairs because they simply haven't saved sufficiently to fund their retirement. They're literally trapped.

I hear from a large number of dentists who are years away from retiring yet can already see the "no end" coming. Worse still, I've heard dentists say, "I only have to keep doing this for another thirteen years, and then I'm finished." It's almost as if they're resigning themselves to thirteen years of pure drudgery, and given the odds, they're still not going to be able to hang up their drills in thirteen years time.

I feel sorry for these dentists. I feel sorry for their staff and for their patients as well. In fact, I feel sorry for all the people who "drudgery dentists" interact with. These poor dentists aren't making the money they want to, so they're unhappy, which means they don't make any more money, because they're unhappy. They have very little job satisfaction, and they've lost the passion for what they do. But dentistry is all they know. They're tied to it by their debts and family obligations. As a result, they're stuck in a quagmire.

There are a number of factors that land dentists in this quagmire. Maybe they've built a dental office around themselves that doesn't attract the best type of people as patients. They may have created an environment that attracts price-conscious patients or people with little respect for their own teeth, people whose dentistry is funded through employer-provided dental insurance and who believe that dentistry is their right, rather than a privilege worth purchasing. Such patients think that because their insurance pays for dental work, they have a right to it. They view their dentists as dental servants, so it's no wonder their dentists end up feeling like slaves to these patients.

Obviously, there's a market out there for dentists who want to treat such patients. And make no mistake, those of the population who barely get by on their income absolutely deserve dental treatment. But dentists who choose to treat mostly these kind of patients will end up being unfulfilled and burned out. Ultimately, they'll be doing a disservice to themselves and to the patients they originally wanted to help.

"But wait," you may be saying, "I don't choose my patients. The market dictates who comes to me."

Well I'm here to tell you that you're wrong.

It's not a matter of what the market dictates. It's a matter of determining which people in that market you want to serve and dedicating your practice to attracting and keeping those people. Any dentist can set up a dental office that attracts the types of patients he or she wants. Unfortunately, the majority of dentists lack either the desire to do so or the knowledge of how to go about it. They don't know, or don't believe, that achieving their dream practice is possible.

Achieving the dental practice of your dreams is possible. I know because I've done it, and once I realized the secret of my success, I decided to share it with others so they too could achieve the success of their dreams. Focusing on this secret is a can't-fail way out of "drudgery dentistry," a first-class ticket, if you will, to both personal and professional fulfillment.

The secret to achieving the dental practice of your dreams is providing The Ultimate Patient Experience for your clients by focusing on top notch, World Class Customer Service.

That's right. A laser-like focus on Customer Service will free you from a life sentence of drilling teeth five or six days a week, fifty weeks out of the year, for years after you're supposed to retire. It will literally buy you time by shortening your workweek and provide you with the financial means to take vacations. And each day that you do work, you'll enjoy the day, every day, until you decide when you want to retire.

Focusing on World Class Customer Service has allowed me, a boy who grew up in a working-class family in the western suburbs of Sydney, to work four days a week, thirty-seven weeks a year, and still collect seven figures annually. It has allowed me to enjoy time with my family and travel the world. And just as importantly, it's allowed me to stay passionate about the dentistry I do and establish rewarding relationships with my staff and the patients we treat. And when I decide the time is right, my focus on

World Class Customer Service will be the reason that I can retire comfortably, when I want to.

The magic of World Class Customer Service and in particular, the magic that is The Ultimate Patient Experience, can establish an incredibly successful Dental Practice for anyone, anywhere. You don't need to practice in a well-heeled area. I was fortunate in my early days as a dentist to work for someone who created a very successful Dental Practice in a community where people were anything but well-to-do, and my own practice was also built by using a Customer Service focus in a community that could also be described as being far from financially wealthy.

I was also very fortunate in other ways too. As I mentioned, I wasn't wealthy. In fact, when my parents built our family home, we lived on bare boards for a couple of years before we had carpet laid. Long before bare boards were fashionable. But they were hardworking people who'd both struggled as children, and they made themselves a better life.

It was drummed into me from an early age by my parents to use my intelligence, and the fact that I was good at school, to create the best possible life that I could for myself.

With their urging and example, I did just that. I didn't want to have to live from paycheck to paycheck. I didn't want to have to ever say, "We can't do that because we can't afford it."

Throughout my school years I had been encouraged to become a doctor, a medico, because of my good grades and my natural problem solving abilities. But I didn't get the grades required for medical school, so I started in dental school at Sydney University with the desire to do my best and see if I could achieve grades that were high enough to get me transferred to the medicine program.

Every day, I took the bus and the train to the University and studied hard, hard enough that I did indeed succeed in being accepted into the medicine program on the basis of my grades in my second year of Dental School. With only three more years of Dental School to go, I made a pivotal decision: I chose to stay in Dentistry. I did this largely because I was becoming tired of being a full-time student. I just wanted to finish studying, get out, and start earning some money and creating a real life for myself.

And I must say my decision to stay on in Dentistry is something I've never regretted.

Although I received very high grades in my first two years of Dental School, I still did not receive any academic awards. So here's what I did. I "throttled back" on the time I spent studying and started working a job in the evenings instead. Toward the end of my degree studies I was working five nights a week in a Servicemen's Club. I tended bar, waited on tables, served patrons at their nightclub, and helped out at rock concerts that were held there.

To support myself through my final years of education, I put in thirty hours a week at the club, working Thursday nights through Monday nights. Very quickly, I learned that the way to be a successful bar attendant and drinks waiter was to provide exceptional service to my patrons—to be friendly and interested in them. As I focused on providing excellent Customer Service, I was able to learn some seriously appropriate people skills. Little did I know what an incredible advantage these skills would give me in my future practice of Dentistry.

Before you assume that my people skills set me up for immediate success when I graduated from Dental School, let me come clean. I was actually "let go" by one of the first dentists I ever worked for. After just one day of working for him, he rang me and told me that they couldn't employ me anymore because I was left handed! He said, "Why didn't you tell me you were left handed?" and I replied, "Well, you didn't ask."

I do recall, however, what this Dentist had told me during my interview for the position. He said, "I've been interviewing so many applicants, and they're all pretty darn boring. You're a standout straight away as a person who can command himself. You're somebody that people can relate to in dentistry." Armed with that strength, off I went to look for another job.

I organized several interviews, scheduling them all on the same day. There was one dental practice with which I hadn't yet scheduled. I'd heard the principal there, Dr. Mike Ahern, was struggling with a bad back, and though I'd called him and spoken with him briefly, he hadn't gotten back to me to arrange a meeting. So on the day of my other interviews, on speck, I dropped in at his office before heading off to the rest of my appointments. When I met Dr. Ahern, it was 9:30 a.m. on a Monday morning and low and behold, there he stood, holding his lower back. He asked me, "Can you stay and start now?"

Obviously, I couldn't. I had other interviews. But at the end of that day, after I'd completed those other interviews, I rang Dr. Ahern back and accepted his position. I started the next day and stayed there for the next three years.

I learned some more people skills and some good lessons in business from working with Dr. Ahern. Dentistry was very good to him, and he was very good to his patients. He was popular, and he readily shared with me some extremely valuable philosophies on dentistry, business, and life. Twenty-eight years later, as I look back on those days, I'm struck by how naïve I was. I had no idea that what I was learning at the time was going to be so impactful and valuable.

So, after three years there, I became eager to take my next steps to success. I bought a Dental Office in a nearby part of Sydney, where residents were mostly working-class. When I purchased my Dental Practice, it was a one man, one auxiliary person operation. The girl who worked there with me answered the phones, took the money, and made the appointments. She mixed the amalgams, cleaned the instruments, and looked after the patients while they were being treated. It was definitely a small dental office. Through my people skills, I was able to attract the right patients and expand quite rapidly: My practice grew from one chair to two chairs and then to four chairs.

I was doing all this expansion mostly out of cash flow; I wasn't accumulating much debt. At that point I knew I was doing something right, but I didn't really appreciate *what* that something right was. I now realize that it was a combination of factors: the brain I'd been born with, the values with which I'd been raised by my parents, the Customer Service focus I'd developed at the club, and the interest in business that I'd acquired from working with my previous employer, Dr. Ahern. All had contributed to my early success. But as that success grew, I was little more than a very busy dentist who knew he had very good people skills and knew he needed extra help. I needed somebody to help with systems and the business of dentistry if my office was to grow from where it had stumbled to by bravado and good fortune to the level I knew it could achieve.

Quite out of the blue, a colleague in dentistry suggested that he could serve as my consultant and provide me with the guidance I needed to take my practice to a whole new level. His suggestion came as a total surprise to me. Though I knew I needed something, I had never considered a colleague's assistance would be the answer. But I knew he'd created a successful practice of his own in another part of town, so I figured, why not? I hired him to be my consultant and went to work on taking my business to that next level.

Being a bit new at the business of dentistry, I was easy to help. And being a bit naïve, I thought my colleague was a miracle worker. After about six months, however, I learned that he was practicing dentistry with another dentist, one mile down the road from me. Yes, he was actually my direct competitor! Sure, he was giving me a little bit of advice here and a little bit of advice there, but he was holding back a lot of the information I really needed to take my practice to the next level. Worse yet, he was using me to test out different strategies, which he'd then tweak and perfect in his own, competing practice.

I know I tend to be too trusting sometimes, but his betrayal hit me like a cold shower. He was someone whose opinion I really valued, someone I thought cared about my family and me. In the end, it turned out I was nothing more than a guinea pig. Fortunately, my optimistic attitude and my ability to see the good in things allowed me to forgive, forget, and move on. Not long afterward, I began working with another consultant.

My new consultant identified the talents I had and told me that being able to relate to people is a significant talent. I already knew that. Any business that can relate to its customers breaks down a lot of barriers and resistances that all business customers have. What I really learned from working with this new consultant was the importance of the consultancy process itself. Getting advice and checking in with my consultant was incredibly helpful to me when it came to the business of dentistry. I'd already recognized that dentistry was a business, but I knew only too well that I hadn't been taught any business skills in dental school. What I'd learned, I'd learned on my own from watching businesses in action through my people-oriented lenses, from listening avidly to other people's experiences, and from reading books. According to my consultant, I'd learned quite a lot that way. But even the best knowledge can benefit from a second pair of eyes and ears when it's applied.

While I was working with that second consultant, I found out that my dentist neighbor was retiring. His dental office was next door to mine, on my floor, right in my same building. So I purchased his practice. I transitioned his patients in with mine, and my business grew immensely, which I put down to one thing: my attention to Customer Service skills. As I gained more and more success by focusing on that aspect, I also realized that I was developing incredibly effective systems all on my own.

My business literally boomed in the years that followed. Over the next five years, my profits doubled. Concurrent with my ever-increasing success, however, I was listening to worries from colleagues all around me: Dentists who were close to burnout from working hard yet not making any money, Dentists who were resigning themselves to a life sentence of drudgery in their dental practices and wondering how they'd ever retire at the age of sixty-five.

In 2007 I was approached to sell my dental practice for a seven-figure amount. It was too smart a business move not to take, so I sold the practice and contracted to continue working on in the practice for another five years. I began to think, "Well, when my contract is up, I'll be fifty-three. What should I do then? Should I stay on longer? Start another dental practice? Do something else entirely?" By that time, I was traveling quite a bit in business circles, and dental speakers and consultants whom I admired very much were encouraging me to step away from the dental chair and to step into the role of becoming a consultant and a speaker myself. Still, I didn't want to stop being a dentist entirely. Once again, I made a choice I'll never regret: I decided to do both. Today I work part-time as a dentist, treating the patients I value so highly. The remainder of my time is devoted to consulting with other dentists, in person or by phone, to help them achieve the success of *their* dreams.

The Business of Dentistry

One of my favorite client calls was from Rachel, who contacted me after reaching out to a number of other consultants. She told me she had a good practice, but she knew she could do better. "I feel like I'm doing all the right things, but I've hit the ceiling. No matter how hard or how long I work, I can't improve my bottom line," she said. "To be honest, some days I think I'm on the verge of burning out. I know I can't keep going this way. I know I need help on the business side, and I know I want to get that help from someone who really knows dentistry."

Less than sixty days after hiring me as her consultant, Rachel was far from burned out. She actually had time to enjoy life outside her practice. And she was again starting to love going to work, as was her staff. Thanks to The Ultimate Patient Experience, her patients clearly loved going to her Dental Practice too. This was because Rachel had blasted through that ceiling she had and increased her monthly collections by more than seventy percent—again, all in *less than sixty days.*

There are a lot of dentists out there like Rachel. They're achieving a certain level of success, but they know it's not the best they can achieve. They know their skills are good. In fact, they're pretty popular. They're not particularly hurting for patients. The problem is they're not maximizing their profits, and they don't want to settle for drudgery dentistry. They don't want to spend one more day of fearing the prospect of working this way until they're sixty-five or older. Nor do they want to spend one day more chasing their tails in their practice, putting away pennies, and living to work rather than working to live. Part of the pleasure of being a dentist is enjoying the lifestyle that goes along with our profession, and dentists like Rachel need to know that they can have an enjoyable lifestyle along the way. They *can* have a practice that will support them in what they want to do now, as well as in retirement.

To achieve all this, these dentists need to develop the mindset that dentistry is not just a craft. Dentistry is a business. The problem is, you don't learn much about business in dental school.

I remember quite clearly the "business" course I took in dental school. It was called Dental Jurisprudence, and it dealt with the legalities of dentistry more than how-to's of running a business. A course in actual business it was *not*. So I know from personal experience that most dentists don't go into practice with the skill set they need to run a dental business successfully, if at all. While it's not their fault that they've failed to achieve the profitability and freedom they deserve, this is no excuse. Help *is* out there when it comes to getting the knowledge you need to achieve the success of your dreams, and you need to go after it. While you can't go out and earn a business degree, you can reach out, as Rachel did, to find a dental business consultant. The trick, of course, is finding the right one.

A large number of dental business consultants have expertise in the area of business, which makes them seem to be a natural choice. After all, you already know dentistry, and they know business. But some of these business consultants have never been dentists themselves, so working with them can be a little difficult for the dentists who are their clients. You see, sometimes, as a dentist, you just want to talk to someone else who's "been there." You need someone who knows what it's like to be working on patients and, at the same time, thinking about the business side. You want another wet-fingered dentist who's been where you are and knows how you're feeling. Sometimes, a non-dentist consultant just does not know the challenges dentists face, and that knowledge of dental practice can be crucial when it comes to overcoming business challenges and achieving success.

Still, having a consultant who's been where you are isn't the whole of it. You also need a consultant whose systems and suggestions can be customized to meet *your* needs. The consultant I worked with, as my practice blossomed, taught me that. He was from a small firm of which the big strength was the ability to tailor advice to different business styles and goals. A dentist friend of mine also used this firm, and though we both had very different practices and very different goals, the consultancy's flexibility allowed it to help both of us achieve a measure of success.

Following six and a half years with this great consultancy, I worked briefly with a consultant who took a far different, one size fits all approach to the business of dentistry. This firmly cemented my conviction that flexibility is vital to a consultant. This consultant's clients were all put through a series of modules. The dentists went through one module for two days, and then the dentists and their teams would go through additional modules over the following six weeks. What's more, several practices went through the modules at the same time. The consultancy entailed, basically, a series of group meetings where we were all herded in to learn the same material all together.

To me, the entire experience was close to useless. I found the modules were teaching me things I already knew, and worse yet, the program didn't take into account the differing or unique needs of the individual dental offices. The most useful thing I took away from this experience was the deep realization that cookie cutter approaches and assembly line learning doesn't work for individualized dental practices.

As both a dentist and a consultant, I've learned what does work: an approach that assesses the needs of a dental practice and gets down to meeting those needs by focusing on World Class Customer Service and delivering an Ultimate Patient Experience. This produces the practice of *your* dreams, not anyone else's. The reason it works is that yes, dentistry is a business, but it's a *people* business. And when you and your staff focus on your patients as people, you establish a mutual relationship of trust that not only brings you the clients you want but also *keeps* those clients with you for the long term.

I've got a great patient named Jeff, who illustrates the strength of this relationship. Jeff and I get along famously. He's been my patient forever, comes regularly, always gets his treatment done, and accepts his treatment plans without question. He's even done electrical work for me at properties I own. I love giving work back to patients whenever I can.

Just recently, we had a small incident during Jeff's last treatment. You see, Jeff has the tongue from hell. All dentists will know what that means. He's got the tongue that's so strong it could probably get its own bronze medal in weight lifting. So here's what happened. While restoring some lower incisal edges for Jeff, I'd been holding The Tongue away with my right hand for what seemed so long that I felt that my right arm would fall off. When his fillings were finally placed and I was able to extricate my right hand from Jeff's mouth, I gave my arm a shake so the circulation could return, and a skerrick of etch that was on my glove flicked under Jeff's safety glasses, right into his eye. We doused the eye vigorously with saline to dilute the etch, and soon the discomfort was gone. No harm done, thank goodness. And to Jeff, it was no big deal. He knew it was a genuine accident, and he wasn't at all angry. He left a happy patient, after making his next appointment, which he kept. That's a testimony to the relationship that Jeff has with our office. Because of The Ultimate Patient Experience, Jeff is family—and he knows it.

Most dental business consultants cover a broad range of topics. As such, they don't "specialize" in Customer Service. They'll mention Customer Service here and there, and maybe, if you're lucky, they'll have a folder on it. They'll go over the contents with you briefly and then declare you properly covered. Truly, I'm a bit too ethical and a bit too invested in my clients' success to promise such a thing. World Class Customer Service is a culture. More importantly, it's an ongoing process. But it's a process that's easy to follow once you get the proper systems and procedures in place. And by delivering an Ultimate Patient Experience, you'll get an enormous return on your investment by noting the following benefits within the first sixty days:

- You'll attract the type of clients you want, patients who'll stay with you for the long haul rather than those who jump from practice to practice, looking for the cheapest rates. And because you're delivering World Class Customer Service, your patients will get a high return on their investment, meaning you can raise your fees above those of practices around you that you once considered competition.

- You'll have a willing, winning team in your office that knows each member is valued and is united in making your patients feel the same way. That's a critical consideration, since dentists themselves spend most of their time with their heads stuck in patients' mouths, which means they've literally got their backs turned on what's going on in their business for most of the business day.

- You'll eliminate time pressures, not only each day but also each week, each month, and each year. We'll expand on smooth daily scheduling and end with how you can shorten your workweek and take regular vacations each and every year.

- You'll have tools in place to make sure you're making the smartest investments for your practice rather than heading deeper and deeper into debt.

- Each moment you spend in your practice will be less stressful and more rewarding. In fact, even weekly meetings will be fun. And when you leave your practice at the end of the day or week, or take vacations, you'll enjoy the lifestyle that you dreamed of back when you were in dental school, that time when you learned everything you needed to know about doing dentistry but absolutely nothing you needed to know about the *business* of running a successful dental practice.

The Best Business Advice I Ever Received

Dr. John Martin, the dentist who sold me his practice in 1987, told me, "The best piece of advice I can give you is to run your business exactly the way you want it, from day one. Choose the days you want to work, from day one, and stick to those, and choose your time off. Don't work six days a week, because all of a sudden you'll be in it for six days a week, and you won't ever be able to get out of it." It was a great piece of advice, because, from day one, I was able to work four days a week. I never felt I needed to work a fifth day, and I maintained that structure throughout my career. It not only lent sanity to my dental practice but it allowed me to live the life outside my business that I wanted to lead.

Dr. Martin also told me, "Set your prices at what you think are best for you and try not to think about what other people are charging. Look at what you think is a fair return on your efforts and your knowledge and your skills and the services that you're providing for your clients." Following that advice allowed me to not only establish fees that brought in the patients I wanted but also allowed me to raise them on a regular basis. And because I was delivering an Ultimate Patient Experience, I didn't lose any patients when I raised my fees.

I'll admit I was lucky to receive such excellent advice early on in my career, but no dentists are doomed to long work hours with low profits because they didn't have Dr. Martin to advise them. Even if you've been in practice for years, you can run your practice the way you want to, starting *right now*.

The Five Most Important Things to Do

People ask me all the time to tell them the top five (or seven, or ten) things they can do to catapult their dental practice to success. The truth is there *aren't* five, seven, or ten most important things. When it comes to creating The Ultimate Patient Experience that will give you the success you deserve, *every* step you take is important. If one person in your dental office is doing one thing wrong, it undoes every good thing that everybody else in your office is doing. No matter whether you're doing five, seven, ten, twenty, or fifty good things, one person in your office breaking the chain lets the whole team down. That's why, when I teach my Ultimate Patient Experience, I get everyone in the practice to focus on procedures with an eye to making them watertight. Every interaction with the patient must be at its optimal best, and the team is committed to continuously making subsequent interactions even better. These connections, these quality interactions, are the core of The Ultimate Patient Experience.

The Best Advice I Have to Give Is to Treat People Better Than You Yourself Want to Be Treated

Going one better than the Golden Rule is the overriding principle behind providing World Class Customer Service. It's also how The Ultimate Patient Experience builds the office culture that cements success. You have to stroke your patients, and you have to stroke your employees. When they do the right thing, praise them and thank them for it. People thrive on praise and thanks. It costs you absolutely nothing to say, "Thanks for turning up on time," or "Thanks for picking up the ball" to a member of your team. It costs you nothing to say to a patient, "Thanks for being a great client. Thanks for sharing that story with me." Yet the rewards of kind statements like this are absolutely priceless.

The bounce-back effect alone will pay you handsomely on a personal level. The more kindness and praise you give out, the better you'll feel for the giving. That's something a lot of people just don't realize in business or in life. There's an instant reward simply for being a giver of praise and a giver of thanks. Matthew McConaughey said it at the Oscars this year. He said, "Gratitude reciprocates!" It makes you a better person.

And then, of course, there's the downstream effect: People you give the praise or thanks to want to spread that good feeling, so they return favor. They pay it forward with kindness to someone else. It's not just a win-win for you and the other person. It's a win win-win for your practice and your world.

The Importance of Continuing (Business) Education

Dentists are devoted to continuing education and admirably so. It's through continuing education courses and seminars that they keep their skills well honed and improve the quality of their dentistry. But when it comes to running a truly successful dental practice, they need to apply that same mindset to the business side. The dentists who have the most successful dental practices are the ones who have read and listened and learned about business from *outside* of

Continued on next page

dentistry and brought that knowledge back to apply it in their dental offices. I believe all dentists who are interested in real success should attend appropriate business seminars, classes, and meetings regularly. There are ample opportunities to do so. In the past seven years alone, I've attended appropriate business events in Chicago (eight times), Arizona (six times), and Nevada (three times). If you're too time pressed to attend such events or don't know where to find them, it's critical to establish an ongoing relationship with a consultant, one who has tapped into the inner circles of business the way you've tapped into the inner circles of dentistry.

Beat Burnout by Giving Back

Unlike dentists who destine themselves to drilling teeth well past the usual retirement age, I could have retired years ago. The big reason I didn't is that practicing dentistry is a privilege, and it's critical to return the privilege by giving back. Not everyone chooses to give back by helping other dentists reach the level of success they deserve. You probably give back to your community and donate to causes you believe in locally, nationally, and globally. You may even give of yourself as a dentist by participating in efforts such as dentistry programs for underserved individuals. Giving of yourself in these ways is a powerful weapon against burnout and drudgery. It reminds you of why you became a dentist in the first place. And when you attain the successful practice you deserve, you can give of yourself in new, fulfilling ways.

I have a patient named Thea, who I've been treating for the last six or seven years without charging her a fee. I'd treated her for ten years before that. You see, seven years ago, Thea said to me, "David, my husband and I have lived too long. We've outlasted our money, and I just can't afford to come and see you anymore." And I said to her, "Thea, it has been my pleasure to have you as a patient for so many years. From now on, it will be my pleasure to treat you free of charge." Now, when Thea comes in, she often says to me, "David, this little repair is costing you money." And I say, "Thea, it's my pleasure." It feels wonderful to be able to give back like that once you're in a healthy position to do so.

Quality over Quantity: Getting the Patients You Really Want

A colleague of mine has a busy office where prospective patients walk in all the time. They show up unannounced to look around, and a fair number of them turn on their heels and leave. A lot of dentists would cringe at the thought of losing all those patients. My friend, on the other hand, is perfectly happy to see them depart.

You see, his office is so well appointed and comfortable it doesn't look like a regular dental office. To many people, it says, "Wow! This is one special place." To others, however, it sends a different message: "This place is going to charge more than I'd planned to spend. I'm getting out of here." That's the reaction of a discount chain customer who walks into Nordstrom's for the very first time. My friend is glad to let those discount shoppers go. He wants the Nordstrom's-style customers, and the wow factor of his beautiful office is attracting the patients he wants in *waves.*

If you ever expect to attain the successful practice of your dreams, you too need to let discount shoppers go. Mark my words, patients who beat you up over price are going to beat you up emotionally time and time again. You don't deserve that! You've studied long and hard and spent a lot of time and money acquiring your dental education and skills. You need to respect that investment by bidding bargain-shopping patients good-bye.

One of the most amazing things about The Ultimate Patient Experience is that it automatically attracts the patients you want. It doesn't attract bargain-shopper patients and, believe me, you don't want them. Granted, there's a huge number of these people out there, patients whose priority is to get the cheapest possible price for their dental work, period. But catering to them is more than a waste of your time. It's a huge a waste of money and a major impediment to achieving the practice of your dreams.

For one thing, it's all but impossible to retain these patients. They're only concerned about getting the lowest possible price they can find, so the minute they find a cheaper dentist, they're gone. For another thing, dental bargain-shoppers are difficult to deal with while you do have them. They tend to want top-level quality in return for the small price they're willing to pay. They'll fight you over every expense, question your every suggestion, and the minute something goes wrong with their dental work because they've cut corners, they'll behave like the customer who bought a discount store coffee pot without bothering to invest in a warranty: they'll raise a huge fuss.

Dental bargain shoppers have what I refer to as an entitlement mentality: "I'm paying for this. You'd better do it for me, and do it right." That's a rather rude mentality that plays out in other unfortunate ways: Dental bargain shoppers will treat your staff poorly no matter how far your staff members go out of their way to help them. And they're always the ones who tap their watch and huff if you're running two minutes behind schedule (though you're expected to "suck it up" when *they* show up fifteen minutes late, of course).

These problem patients do *nothing* to help your bottom line and, in fact, do a great deal to hurt it. They drain you and your staff and waste your resources, which leaves you literally bleeding money. Plus, their antics can alienate the patients you really want. Providing an Ultimate Patient Experience in your practice with World Class Customer Service is all about making your patients feel comfortable and valued. Embarrassing behavior from one patient can ruin the entire experience for all of your other patients. It's hard for anyone to watch someone huff, puff, and complain without wondering whether that's the sort of person the staff and clients have to put up with every day. And let's be honest. Would you want a dentist to work on you after dealing with a problem patient? An embarrassing scene certainly doesn't leave the dentist or the dental team in the best frame of mind, does it?

As a very wise friend once told me, life is too short to deal with nasty people. I, for one prefer pleasant, profitable days. Cheapskate patients are an obstacle to a pleasant, profitable practice, so you have to let them go. That's actually pretty easy to do, since if you stop chasing them, they'll actually end up leaving on their own.

The key is to focus on the patients you want instead: long-term, regular patients who value quality and give you the loyalty that Nordstrom's gets from its customers. When it comes to dentistry, these people want to take care of their teeth, and when problems arise with a tooth, they want to keep that tooth. The beauty of such patients is that they're far less demanding and far more gracious and appreciative than discount shoppers are. They *enjoy* investing their money in things that give them a good return on their investment. They're willing to pay a substantially higher than average fee in return for the substantially higher than average services you provide.

The Gift of Customer Service Eyes

Providing an Ultimate Patient Experience involves looking at your practice through what I call Customer Service Eyes, which means paying attention to every detail that will enhance each and every one of your patients' experiences. At first glance though, the details you have to examine can seem overwhelming. But once you get the hang of it, what's required really becomes second nature.

An interesting article came across my desk the other day. It was written by a woman who, without intending to, summed up really well what I mean by Customer Service Eyes.

She was talking about successful dating and how she would always pay attention on the first date to how the gentleman who took her out would interact with the wait staff. She would then decide whether she would continue the relationship with this gentleman based on their behavior. If he was attentive and kind and pleasant to the wait staff, she knew she could expect him to treat her the same way, and she'd agree to go on a second date. However, if he was rude and arrogant and ignorant of the wait staff, she was done. She felt that his ignorant behavior was a reflection of his inner self. If he was concentrating so much on himself that he failed to treat the wait staff as actual human beings, she wasn't going to waste her time on him.

Continued on next page

Having Customer Service Eyes makes you see things from your clients' perspectives in much the same way. You become focused on your patients as people, not just as dental cases. To have this focus—to think and care about what your patients need as human beings—is to look at the world through Customer Service Eyes.

The fabulous thing about these eyes is that each time you use them, your eyesight gets keener. Your whole mindset becomes one of wanting to improve your patients' experiences and upping the *WOW* factor each time they come for treatment.

The real gift of excellence that Customer Service Eyes gives you is the ability to always be looking at every aspect of your Dental Office, knowing that there is always room to improve on everything that you do and everything that you have done, each and every time before.

The Environment That Gets You the Patients You Want

Now that you've decided that you want to attract Nordstrom's-style customers, let's look at the physical environment of your office through Customer Service Eyes. If you open those eyes, you'll easily see how the ambience you create helps attract and keep the type of patients you want.

In an Ultimate Patient Experience world—that is, a truly World Class Customer Service world—every aspect of your practice is devoted toward building a relationship with your patient. Dentistry actually becomes secondary to that relationship. What is primary is to make your patient always feel as welcome and as valued as if they were a guest in your home. This means that you're aiming for your office ambience to be equal to or better than that of a top-notch attorney or successful finance firm, not a run-down old doctor's office with a waiting room full of bench seats. In fact, dental practices that offer an Ultimate Patient Experience don't have *waiting* rooms at all. They have client lounges.

A client lounge is all about comfort and relaxation, so it needs attractive, comfortable furniture for your clients to relax in. It also needs lighting that sets a warm mood, nice lamps rather than harsh overhead fluorescents. To further set the mood, there's nice, pleasant background music. Easy listening or classical is always a good choice. Under no circumstances should the radio be playing. Even if you don't advertise on the radio, your competition might, and having your clients listen to your competition's ads while they sit in your office just doesn't make any sense.

As for TV, be selective about the message it sends. One of my consulting clients recently told me how one day he had the US Masters golf live on the TV in his client lounge on a day when his appointments were running behind. He had had a difficult extraction to do, and his book was a bit jammed up. When he greeted his next patient, who had been waiting a while now, that patient was livid. The patient said, "You can't keep me waiting like this while you're sitting back there watching the golf!" My client replied, "I'm not watching the golf. I've been working my tail off back there!" But his patient wouldn't believe him, because that TV had sent the wrong message.

I recommend running the TV in your client lounge with the sound turned off. The television in my own practice plays either slideshows of lovely travel scenes or educational videos that feature images of modern dental processes. For example, I have a video from Invisalign that I like to run, since it shows the technology in a way that's upbeat and interesting but doesn't feature photos that are unattractive. I would never run a video showing boring before and after pictures of bad teeth and good teeth, or dirty mouths and clean mouths.

Nor would I put on a regular TV channel. It will be a turn-off for patients who don't like the program, be it news, a sitcom, or a cooking show. Turn-offs aren't exactly welcoming.

Magazine choices are much like television. You should always put the message they send to your patient above matters of personal interest. Magazines in your client lounge shouldn't be the old issues of magazines that you just finished reading at home. Try to avoid specialized publications on things such as golf or guns. And, by all means, avoid anything that's tattered and old. There's actually a Seinfeld joke on this topic: "What's the difference between a dentist and a sadist? The sadist has newer magazines."

Your client lounge should be stocked with new magazines that cater to the general interests of the patients you want: luxury, coffee table publications such as *Travel & Leisure, Harper's Bazaar, Gourmet Traveler,* and *Town & Country*. I've had dentists disagree with me on this, claiming such magazines are their competition because if their patients spend money on travel and fine dining, they won't spend money on dentistry. But remember you're no longer chasing after patients who are so focused on price that they wonder if they should take care of their teeth or vacation in the Bahamas. To the patients you want, good magazines indicate that your world is their world; you appreciate the same things. That's the kind of message that builds and strengthens relationships.

Please Steal Our Magazines!

Actually, we'll give them to you. I detest stickers that read, "Property of XYZ Dental" plastered all over dental office magazines. Using stickers in this way is pretty much the same as saying, "We know you're paying thousands of dollars for your treatment, but we can't have you stealing our five-dollar magazines." That's a really bad message that a lot of offices don't realize that they're sending to their clients. I prefer to use magazines to best advantage by encouraging patients to take them home. If patients in my client lounge have their heads in a magazine when a team member comes out to take them back for treatment, my team member is instructed to say something like, "Oh, you're reading something good there? Bring it with you, and you can take it home." By doing so, we're using the law of reciprocity to play a big role in building and strengthening our relationships with our patients: you give me something, I give you something in return, and we both end up feeling good about it. The law of reciprocity means you're getting a big return on that $5.00 magazine by giving it away.

Signs of Trouble, Posters of Doom

Looking at your office through Customer Service Eyes leaves no detail missed, no stone unturned. So let's turn over a big one now and look at what's hanging on your walls and how it's weighing you down.

I'm betting the walls of your waiting room, as well as your front office and treatment rooms, bear a fair amount of what you view as "good information" in the form of signs, posters, before and after photos of dental work, and marketing or advertising materials. You need to take them down and replace them with tasteful artwork, photos of stunning landscapes, and similar visual treats. Trust me. The messages sent by anything else can alienate the patients you want to attract.

Some signs in your office may be required by law, such as those that indicate exits and handicapped entrances. And a very few may be necessary for things such as designating the difference between the men's and women's restrooms. But beyond that, you don't need signs for instructional purposes. If you don't put them up for guests in your home, why would you put them in your warm, welcoming office? In general, signs are rude, especially for the clients that *you* have chosen. Those clients wouldn't think of answering their cell phone and babbling loudly in the lounge. They won't solicit you during business hours. And if "payment must be made *in full* at time of service" is your policy, your patients should already know this. The mere hint that your valued patient would fleece you, let alone the presence of a sign that shouts it out, is indeed alienating in the extreme.

Surveys have established that one of the major reasons people leave a dental practice is because they don't like being lectured to. That's exactly what dental posters do when they declare, "GOOD HYGIENE IS IMPORTANT" and "DENTAL DECAY CAN SHORTEN YOUR LIFE." These sort of posters lecture the readers, patronizing them and making them feel decidedly uncomfortable about themselves. That creates a direct conflict with the welcoming, comfortable ambience that you want to create.

What's especially alarming about these posters is that they usually include nasty-looking photos of decayed teeth and diseased gums, images so unpleasant that no "after" images of gleaming teeth and joyous smiles can compensate for their unpleasantness. I've even seen dentists who have themselves taken nasty "before" photos of their patients and proudly posted them on the office walls (paired with perfect smiles above or below them, of course). This is anything but good marketing in the world of The Ultimate Patient Experience. Nothing is more unsettling for your patient than staring at photos of bad teeth before their dental work is done. It doesn't matter how beautiful you think the "afters" look. It's the "befores" that speak more loudly to your patients, and the discomfort these "before" photos can cause will scare away the patients you want.

What about other marketing materials? You know, the flyers or brochures in wall racks that tell your patients about how great someone else's product or technology is? If you read the last sentence carefully, you'll notice the contradiction within. Other people's marketing doesn't belong in your office, unless it's personally handed to a patient you feel is a candidate for a specific product or technique. Even in such cases, I advise being very selective about the type of products you share.

I also advise selectivity when posting materials that tell your patients how wonderful you are. Other than a few items that support your professional qualifications (such as framed copies of your credentials and certificates of truly outstanding recognition you've received), these can come off as tacky and degrading. At best, they send messages that your patients should not need to be reading. It's the experience you're giving them that matters. If you're providing the Ultimate Patient Experience that they came for, telling them how wonderful you are when you should be *showing* them this is silly. And if you're not giving them a total experience that conveys how much you care about them, no lovely certificates of your professional achievements will ever possibly compensate.

One final word about the ambience in your office: beware of "check-in counters," especially those with sliding glass windows. I don't want to give you the impression that creating the right ambience requires a major renovation or reconstruction, especially since one of the big pluses about creating The Ultimate Patient Experience is that it's all about *service*, so it's not an expensive proposition at all. But setups in which the patient "reports in" to a receptionist behind glass and gets handed a clipboard with paperwork to complete and then gets dismissed are really something you want to avoid. They set an ambience that's somewhat akin to visiting someone in prison, and they create an automatic separation between your patient and your dental team. When offering an Ultimate Patient Experience, you want to constantly *connect* your staff and your patients, so those patients get full advantage from meeting and connecting with your winning team.

3

Creating a Winning Team

Far too many dentists start their day the same way: They walk into their office around 9:00 a.m., give their staff members a perfunctory nod, and go straight to the treatment room. Within ten minutes they have their heads stuck in someone's mouth, thinking not about that someone as a person but only about those teeth. Meanwhile, that dentist's staff members start trickling in while the dentist and a few other staff members are already working. The team members wander in and go to their respective workstations without bothering to greet other members of the staff. Those who enter from the back never come up to greet the others in the front and vice versa. All around the dentist, balls are being dropped. While the dentist is working on one patient, other patients are already waiting. No one has greeted those patients properly. The staff members are too busy sipping their coffee and firing up their computers. New patient calls are being flubbed because the person whose job it is to answer those calls is late or busy elsewhere. Everyone in the office is in their own headspace, and nobody is truly focused on meeting the patients' needs.

What these dentists don't know is that all those dropped balls have destined him and his staff for a disorganized, unfulfilling, and highly unprofitable day, all before the clock even hits 9:15 a.m.

In a dream dental practice, the day starts differently. A core team comes in to open the office at least thirty minutes before the dentist appears. The team members turn on the lights, the computers, the equipment, and the music. When the dentist arrives, they all then have a brief morning huddle meeting to go over the expectations of the day: who's coming in, what treatments are being performed on those people, and what needs to be readied for all of those patients.

If they're good team members, they have already taken care of most of the preparation already on the day before. They're not walking into what I call a cold setup, in which the person who runs the front office has to ask, "Now, what do we need to do first?" The front office staff members already know what's going on for the day, as do the other members of the core team. They have checked the schedule and prepared for this morning's patients on the afternoon before. They now go over things in the morning huddle to make *sure* all is in readiness, in the same way that any good sports team goes over its opening plays before the game begins.

That's when you arrive to be there for the morning huddle so you and your morning team can discuss the flow of the day. You greet your staff warmly and politely and tell them you're looking forward to the day. Why wouldn't you? You're working with a winning team.

Leading by Example from the Day's Very Start

As the head of your team, you lead by example. That's particularly important when leading a winning team. Winning team members are pleasant and courteous to each other as well as to their patients, so you need to be friendly and courteous to your team. Greet them warmly each morning and tell them you're looking forward to a wonderful day. Say, "Please" and "Thank you" and "You're welcome" to them as they perform their daily duties, and always thank them warmly and genuinely for their help at the end of each and every day.

And smile!

Another great way to set an example is to arrive at least twenty minutes before your first appointment of the day. Doing so makes your team's job easier, since early morning patients tend to arrive even earlier than their scheduled appointment time. Dentists who don't time their arrival accordingly can show up *after* the patient does. I see a lot of this. A dentist will walk in at five past nine for a 9:00 a.m. appointment, when the patient has already been sitting there since a quarter to nine. Keeping that customer waiting not only sends the message that the customer is not a top priority but also creates a massive disruption from the day's very beginning. Suddenly, everyone is in "rush mode" instead of in the steady flow that you need to establish early on and maintain through the balance of the day.

Continued on next page

Your final requirement in setting an example is being "in the zone" when you walk through the door. Your mindset, your words, and even your posture should all send the message that you're ready and eager to go. You're not worried about what happened at the dinner table last night or the hassles you may have already encountered before you arrived at the office that morning. You leave that all behind because you expect your team to do the same. You show up focused, with a positive manner, because you expect these things from your team too. Your example shows your team that you are all on the same page. It not only sets the tone for the morning but it also goes a long way toward achieving an ultra-productive day.

The Madness of Micromanagement

Micromanagement is one of the biggest mistakes I see in dental practices today. It's a major reason why dentists stay trapped in drudgery. You see, a lot of dentists feel that they need to be the ones filling out all the lab slips, doing all the ordering, keeping track of stock, and even doing payroll. They're micromanaging: micromanaging the stock control, micromanaging the payroll, etc. The list goes on. Having your hands in everything is a surefire way to burn out. It's also a surefire way of hurting your bottom line.

The odds are that your micromanaging tendencies started out with the best of intentions. It's only natural to want to do everything yourself in order to make sure that it's all done properly. But there is no way that dentists can do all of these tasks. If you try to juggle too many tasks in your practice, balls will definitely get dropped. Eventually, you reach that all too familiar point where you know you're a good dentist, and you know you're giving your practice the lion's share of your time, but you also know that there has to be a better way.

That better way is to stop micromanaging and give your staff the opportunity to become a truly excellent team.

Winning teams are common in businesses that have an excellent corporate culture, such as Zappos, Starbucks, and Chick-fil-A. Each of these businesses is dramatically different from the others. Their common denominator is that all employees feel valued for the work they do. They feel trusted and respected, and these feelings are at the core of what makes each of them winning teams. When you micromanage your team, those feelings don't develop. How could they, when your micromanaging tells your team members that you need to look over their shoulder to make sure things are being done correctly? You don't trust them to do things the right way.

Micromanagement has an absolutely lethal impact on World Class Customer Service, which, if I might remind you, values your patients as people and gives them what they need. The distrust inherent in micromanagement devalues the people who work for you. It deprives them of the motivation and respect that *they* need to succeed. I'm willing to bet you that they don't deserve that. If you've achieved the level of success that has allowed you to pick up this book, you can't have a truly terrible team. What you have is a team that needs top-notch procedures that motivate and set the stage for success.

If you want a winning team, staff members who have a passion for their work and a passion for the customers they're serving, then you have to loosen your grip on micromanagement and give your staff what they really need to do their jobs. That means putting procedures in place that enhances communication, eliminates isolation, and strengthens relationships between all members of your team.

The Winning Way to Start Your Day

The best way to start your day is to begin with longer productive appointments. We'll talk about the perfect way to schedule appointments throughout the day in a later chapter, but morning appointments are so important that they're worth touching on here. What you don't want is to walk in to a series of short fifteen minute appointments first thing in the morning, where every chair is tied up with people needing orthodontic adjustments, denture try-ins, and fissure sealants. This makes for a lot of washing up and a lot of switching of duties and handoffs between you and your team. The resulting traffic jam can leave everyone rushing around, feeling hurried and hassled. That's not the sort of start that you want for your day.

Instead, making sure you start your day with a longer procedure, like a crown impression or an implant, is optimal for two reasons: Firstly, a productive appointment (meaning one that's highly profitable) gets the practice off to a good financial start for the day. That's a weight off your mind as the dentist, which helps you set a positive tone for the day. Secondly, a long appointment will keep only the doctor and a few other team members occupied, so the rest of the team members can get a running start on their own duties for the day.

The Power of Pinch-Hitting

In your dream practice, you don't do drudgery. You're out of that trap because you're not trying to do it all. Your role is to perform the dentistry, oversee the business, and let your winning team do the rest. But a winning team isn't composed of players who work in isolation. It's made up of people who naturally huddle, not just in the morning but many times during the day. They may not stand shoulder to shoulder, but they're constantly communicating with each other and always with the benefit of the customer in mind. They respect one another, because they know that each member of the team has an important role to play. And to win the game one customer at a time, they learn each others' positions and develop each others' skills. Each team member has another that they can tag-team with. That way if one player gets pulled out of place, the field is still covered. There's always someone there who will be able to pick up the ball.

I see an awful lot of dentists who, out of necessity, have a large staff. After all, there are a lot of jobs to be done. But what saddens me is seeing each of these jobs being done by a single person in virtual isolation. There's a certain territoriality that reigns in these dental practices: Everyone performs their own duties with no knowledge of how they fit into the big picture and no desire to know. For example, there's an insurance person who does that job exclusively but has no idea how a great appointment book is run. And there's a financial coordinator who takes the money but has no idea how payroll is organized. Unfortunately, this degree of specialization and isolation is far more detrimental to the function and the performance of the whole office than you would possibly know.

I'm sure you've undoubtedly encountered some of the problems that occur when everyone in your office is assigned to their own specialized, isolated tasks. You've walked into the office only to be told, "Oh, yeah. Robyn's daughter is sick today. So Robyn's not coming in. So, we can't make any crown appointments, because she's the only one who knows where the lab work is." And I'm betting you've become so resigned to such scenarios that you just wait until Robyn returns to the office and let her deal with the delays her absence has caused.

The problem is that your patients also have to deal with these delays, and if World Class Customer Service is your focus, then this just can not happen. Customer Service that hinges on how quickly Robyn's daughter recovers from a tummy bug isn't exactly setting the standard for World Class quality.

Now imagine that Robyn, who's in charge of the lab orders, coordinates crown appointments with Clarissa, the team member who's already in charge of scheduling. If Robyn is a great member of your team, she's shared information with Clarissa about how the lab work is tracked. And Clarissa, being a great team member herself, has shown an interest in that process. Therein lies the opportunity for excellence: Once Robyn identifies Clarissa's interest, she can then train her in the processes required. And when Robyn calls in because her daughter is sick, Clarissa is there to pick up the ball. She checks the status of the lab work and schedules the crown appointments accordingly. Neither the office nor the patients suffer any delays. It probably never occurred to you to empower the Robyn in your office to identify an interest expressed by your Clarissa, let alone cultivate that interest to show Clarissa the ropes required. And that's the point: Most dentists don't know how to manage their offices for maximum Customer Service success. They don't allow Robyn to assume that level of control because they prefer to micromanage. Seriously micromanaging dentists tend to choke really good employees, when those employees could leap from being really good to being truly excellent if given the opportunity.

As a consultant, I strongly believe that every office has a person who excels at every practice duty. It is critically important to identify and recognize each of these employees, but it is equally as important to make them responsible for ensuring they have a pinch-hitter who can do each and every one of their tasks just as well. The goal is to empower those wonderful people to empower other wonderful people, and in doing so, build a wonderful team.

Even if you never considered allowing your employees to work this way, you're already seeing the beauty of such a system, aren't you? Maybe you have somebody who can do everything at the front desk well: They're great at scheduling appointments, great at collecting money, and great at dealing with insurance. But that somebody still has to take sick days. They still have to take vacation time and take daily lunch breaks. If you have other team members who can do each of those front desk tasks just as well, the ball is *never* dropped. When the front desk person is out to lunch, the staff member the front desk person has trained can come up from the back and schedule Mrs. Smith's next appointment as well as take care of her billing and insurance details. Mrs. Smith doesn't even know she's being handled by a pinch-hitter. All she knows is that her needs are being taken care of in a warm, efficient, seamless way. Mrs. Smith wins, and when she wins, the rest of your office wins as well.

Pinch-hitting is only one procedure that can transport a team from good to excellent. We'll touch on other winning procedures throughout the balance of this book. But pinch-hitting is the one I use as a shining example because it's one of the fastest ways to boost efficiency and teamwork. The energy created as team members communicate closely and develop new skills is infectious. It grows quickly as joint efforts pay off with less stressful days, more satisfied patients, and increased opportunities to take time off. What's more, it builds a culture of mutual respect. Now that team members are no longer working in isolation, they understand every link in the chain that makes up your team. Team members gain an appreciation for everyone else's job, not just their own. Everyone, including you, *enjoys* coming to work.

"My Staff Won't Let Me Do That"

I've found a lot of dentists out there who use this excuse in regard to new procedures, simply because they underestimate their team. I love to show these dentists that they're wrong. I've seen good teams become great ones and so-so teams become downright dreams when micromanagement stops and empowering procedures start. By and large, people want to excel; they want to do work that has meaning and purpose, and they want to do it well. Using World Class Customer Service to provide an Ultimate Patient Experience is a goal that clearly has meaning and purpose, and team members respond admirably when united by that goal. True, you may encounter some discomfort among your staff when you first put new procedures in place. If you've chosen the right people for your team, it's a very simple matter to deal with this discomfort before you encounter out-and-out resistance. You just need to exert a little authority.

I mention this because I've had Dentist clients who've told me "My staff will never go for this" for a second reason: Not because these Dentists underestimate their team but because they underestimate *themselves.* They've lost the authority to manage their own practices. And to lead a winning team, they need to get that authority back.

Sometimes the signs that dentists have lost authority are clear: They tolerate people who come in late, people who come in ungroomed, with their hair still wet, and people who come in only to start making their breakfast at work. If you have such red flags within your practice, they have to be corrected immediately. Professionalism and proficiency are absolute requirements for *every* member of a winning team and especially its leader. Failure to exercise authority when lapses occur is a failure to do the job you signed up for when you committed to World Class Customer Service. Set an example like that, and you'll lose the respect of a would-be winning team.

Other authority problems are harder to spot because dentists have willingly handed over authority to certain team members for years and years. In doing so, they've created some bad apples. They've created control freaks. Control freaks are strong-willed individuals who are totally in charge of the jobs they do and are usually very good at those jobs. That's why dentists let them do their thing without ever managing them; they seem like such big assets to the team. The thing is, control freaks are only in charge of what they want to be in charge of, and they only do things the way they want to do them. Faced with the prospect of doing things another way, or sharing, or pinch-hitting, control freaks can balk big time, even to the point of challenging your authority.

Luckily, there's an easy way to turn a control freak into a true asset, and it's a process that nips resistance to change while upping excellence *throughout* your team. It's the process of training.

Full Team Training

No task in a practice that provides The Ultimate Patient Experience can be allocated to anyone who is not properly trained for it. Too many dentists consider the use of untrained team members to be normal and acceptable in the usual course of business, when it's anything but.

I see the fallout from lack of training far too often. For example, a member of the clinical team is "thrown" onto the front desk to answer the phone and handle appointments without being fully trained in these tasks. This person bobbles the ball and inconveniences your patients, undercutting World Class Customer Service in a big way.

Think about it. Why should your patients have to play roulette when they call or do business with your office? Why should they ever have to deal with someone who is undertrained and a weak link, yet still be expected to pay full price for that service or process? It just wouldn't be fair. After all, you wouldn't expect to be served a meal at a fine dining restaurant by a sous chef who'd been pressed into wait staff duty on ten minutes' notice. Nor would you feel safe knowing that your car was serviced by the kid who usually washes the cars simply because the regular auto mechanic was not available that day. Your patients need fully trained individuals on your team. It's your responsibility to provide that necessary training to all of your team.

The training process for creating an Ultimate Patient Experience practice is incredibly eye opening to my dentist clients. It makes everyone on your team more comfortable with making changes, right down to a would-be control freak. The process of training also helps you, the team leader, spot strengths in your people that you didn't even know they had. For another thing, it makes everyone less likely to resist change and enjoy the process, even a control freak. But the greatest thing to watch is how people blossom when they're trained this way. It empowers them to live up to their potential. It shows them that their roles and those of other team members matter more to the practice than they ever realized. It does more than increase their value to your practice; it makes them feel valued as people. And a team that feels that way will make sure your patients feel the same way.

The Onboard Terrorist

I read in a dental social media forum where a dentist bemoaned:

> *"I had a toxic employee for over two decades. If you let time go by without doing anything about it, it becomes a normal part of your practice. It probably was my worst mistake in my thirty-three years in practice to keep such a negative member in my practice."*

Two decades? It's a wonder that dentist still had a practice at all!

Continued on next page

In 2008 I learned a title for this kind of employee that seemed most apt. And the reason it seemed most apt was because, at that time, in my office, we had a toxic staff member who had been with us for some two or three years. That title for that employee was that she was an "onboard terrorist", a term I learned in a class I took on charismatic leadership. The class centered on leadership styles, but at the time, that "terrorist" term was my big takeaway.

In the dental office, an onboard terrorist is an employee who is entirely with the program on the surface but, behind the scenes, deliberately brings your whole business down. This type of individual appears to be working with the team to achieve the common goal but in the background, for whatever reason, is severely and deliberately sabotaging the organization.

Typically, onboard terrorists are good employees. They demonstrate genuinely good business characteristics for a reasonable amount of the time. However, when they switch to terrorist mode, their negative effect on your business seriously outweighs any good they seem to be doing.

Onboard terrorists are snakes. Discovery, identification, and removal of these snakes is absolutely critical to your practice.

In my 2008 terrorist case, the employee in question was sabotaging the front office. This employee was behaving

Continued on next page

and speaking to patients and customers in a manner that totally undid all of the great work being done by everyone else who interacted with those patients. The front office is the patient's final touch point in The Ultimate Patient Experience, so it's especially key in reinforcing the positivity that's already been created during the patient's visit. A terrorist who creates a negative experience will override and destroy all the wonderful work established by the rest of the dental office team.

A dental office is too small an environment not to have every employee 100 percent onboard. Team members who aren't acting in the best interests of the business and the office will succeed in bringing down the morale of the team members who are on board, so terrorists must be identified and dealt with.

The reasons that an employee decides to become an onboard terrorist aren't always obvious. Nor do they need to be. There's no excuse for terrorist behavior. None. Sadly, as in the case of true terrorism, there is no redemption. The terrorist must be excised and removed from your office. A leopard never changes its spots. A snake is a snake is a snake.

Allowing the terrorist to prevail threatens your credibility and authority. If you fail to act quickly to remove a known terrorist, you'll be seen as weak, ineffectual, and unfair by your team. Conversely, excising the terrorist will elevate your reputation

Continued on next page

in the eyes of the rest of your team members. And in so doing, it will also elevate your team.

One of the key obstacles that business owners encounter with terrorists is the fear that their team can't survive without them. That's why, as in our friend's case mentioned above, some dentists hang on to their onboard terrorist for way too long. Dismiss that concern. Truth is, your team is being victimized as long as that terrorist is in their midst. Your team will survive when the snake is removed. In fact, they'll thrive. When I removed my onboard terrorist, the entire team rallied and stepped up to the plate. Life went on. Not as usual, but better—much, much better than before.

If you have a terrorist occupying space on your team or in your head, you need to remove that terrorist and move on. Nothing else works as well. In fact, nothing else works at all.

Creating the Ultimate Connection

The other day my wife, Jayne, who works in my dental office with me, phoned a colleague of mine who I'll call Dr. Jones. Dr. Jones had given our office a particular dental supply to try, and Jayne needed to know where to order more of that product. Here's how the phone call went:

Ring. Ring.

"Hello."

Jayne: "Hello? Is this Dr. Jones' office?"

Answer: "Yes, it is."

Poor Dr. Jones. The young lady he had assigned to answer his phone had such disrespect for her duties that she didn't even identify his office upfront.

Jayne explained to the young lady, who we'll refer to as Kelly, exactly why she was calling. She described the product in question and asked for the name of the dental supply company that provided it.

To which Kelly replied, "Oh I wouldn't have a clue. Dr. Jones does all the ordering here."

Sadly, too much information here. If Dr. Jones chooses to manage his stock himself, that's his business, not ours. Personally, I delegate that duty, for reasons I've already explained. But even if I didn't, that's not the sort of information I want blurted around.

Secondly, the use of the phrase, "I wouldn't have a clue," is not good. By its very nature, it sounds disrespectful.

My wife asked Kelly to kindly look up the information. As Kelly began her search, another phone line in Dr. Jones' office began to ring.

It rang, and it rang, and it rang. And it continued to ring while Kelly ignored it.

Finally, Jayne threw her a rope. "Kelly, do you want to answer that other line?"

"No," Kelly said. "It's okay."

My wife replied, "No, Kelly, it's not okay. You need to answer that phone."

Kelly answered, "It's okay. They'll call back."

By the time Jayne could say, "Kelly, you really need to take that call," it was too late. The phone had stopped ringing. The caller had given up.

I feel sad for Dr. Jones. He probably has no idea that his phone is being answered so poorly, with such disregard for his patients and his practice. Or maybe he knows, but he doesn't care.

That makes me sadder still, because he would definitely care if he knew exactly how much those mismanaged calls were costing him.

The All Important First Call

The quickest way for me, as a consultant, to improve my dental clients' bottom lines is to teach the entire staff better phone skills. I have a number of techniques that fine-tune the phone skills needed in an Ultimate Patient Experience dental office, and I could write a book on these techniques alone. For this book, however, we'll map out the first patient call, because the very first call from a prospective patient is the first step in creating what I call The Ultimate Connection, a series of personal interactions that build an unshakable relationship between your new client and your office.

Doctors, do you know how many people ring your office with a new-patient inquiry and how many of those callers you convert to an appointment? You should know, since, for every new patient call that *isn't* converted, you're actually losing what I call free money. Most dental offices are only converting one out of five calls. If they can lift that number up to two out of five, they've doubled their number of new patients. And we all know how much a new patient is worth in our practice, on average. So every call you don't convert lets that money slip away—and that's free money.

As I tell people in first-call training, the public isn't sitting around at home with time on their side, thinking they might just pick up the phone and start calling dental offices for fun. They're actually phoning your office because they have a specific dental problem, and they've already decided they *want you* to solve it. They're looking for confirmation that you recognize their problem, sympathize with them, and *want* to help them. They're looking for a friend, and your role is to always—always!— be that friend.

Thirty years ago, calls were more complicated. People chose their dentists from the Yellow Pages, starting with the As and working through to Z. That's all they had to go on: what your name was and how it sounded. So when they called, they really had no other choice than to ask questions, and often, a lot of questions. But in this day and age, people do their research before they call you. They've checked your website and bought into your marketing and advertising. They've *bought in*. They've already determined that they want you to do their dentistry by the time they pick up the phone. So, to turn that first call into a new patient, the following conversation needs to happen:

Ring, ring.

The call is answered immediately.

"Thank you for calling Dream Dental. This is Jenny. How may I help you?"

The odds are high that Jenny will get a question like "How much do you charge for a filling/cleaning/check-up?" It's the number one question prospective patients ask, as you may already know. But I know the number one reason that new callers ask about price first: they simply have no other point of reference. With this fact in mind, Jenny's number one priority is to make the question of price irrelevant by convincing the caller that your dental practice is the best one to take care of them. If they then choose to go elsewhere for their dentistry, they do so knowing they've compromised their choice.

So Jenny answers that question with several questions of her own.

"When were you last in to see us?"

Leading with this question immediately allows Jenny to control the conversation and gather vital information without offending the caller, who could actually be a regular patient who was just in the office the day before. In such a case, the classic question, "Are you a patient of Dr. Moffet's?" leaves the caller feeling like a meaningless stranger. And should the caller state that she's not yet a patient, Jenny can ask her name and then say, "Which one of our valued patients can we thank for recommending our dental office to you, Mrs. Adams?" Translation: "We value our patients, welcome new patient referrals, and reward our existing patients who refer clients to us."

Once Jenny has established this, she can ask, "How long has it been, do you think, since you last went to the dentist?"

It's probably been a while, so Jenny moves on.

"Can you give me your e-mail address? I'd like to send you out our special report, titled *Fifteen Reasons Why Smart People Put Off Going to the Dentist and How Those Decisions Are Affecting Our Health and Driving Us Prematurely into Our Graves.*

"While I'm writing your e-mail address down, can I also please have your mobile phone number, just in case we are cut off? You know, my sister was cut off yesterday while standing on the top of a hill. Can you believe that?"

The brilliance of this chatty yet professional approach is that Jenny is continuously strengthening the connection between herself and her caller. She's showing she cares, and she's being a friend. And while she's at it, she's deflected the cost question so deftly that it's gone right out of Mrs. Adams' mind. By the time Jenny has finished talking with Mrs. Adams about her needs and her filling, they've become good friends. When Jenny asks Mrs. Adams if she prefers a morning or an afternoon appointment, Mrs. Adams is sold. She's become a new patient of the practice.

How to Blow a Conversion Call

"Have you been here before?"

"I don't know that."

"You need to come in for an exam before we can answer that question."

"It depends."

None of these statements should ever be uttered to any of your prospective clients, or to existing patients, for that matter. They serve only to close down communication with the caller and give no feedback about the excellent care you and your dental office offer. If your phone is answered with these poor answers, or other answers that are just as poor, the caller is left to judge your office only on your receptionist's less than World Class phone manner. That's a lose-lose situation. You miss out on a new patient, and the patient misses out on the quality dentistry and The Ultimate Patient Experience that your office is famous for providing.

Continued on next page

In *The Wolf of Wall Street*, Jordan Belfort turned a ragtag staff into a team of millionaires by making sure his team stuck to the systems he put in place. In your Dental Office, you're actually in a much better position, since you don't have a ragtag team. If you did, you wouldn't have become successful enough to be interested in my book. All you need to do to reach the next level is put the proper telephone answering protocols in place and train your team to follow them. For clients of mine, that's an easily attainable goal.

How to ***Not*** Cancel an Appointment

Dream dental offices have a strict mindset about cancellations: they simply cannot occur. Every cancellation that happens creates way more work for everyone in the office, and this means you're losing money. To avoid this trap, team members excel at making appointments, and they also excel at ensuring those appointments are kept.

My wife is a master at this. Recently, a patient called on a Monday to say he couldn't make his Friday appointment. She said to him, "That's all right, John. I can get you in sooner." Suddenly, John was able to keep his appointment on Friday.

Most of the time, people's reasons for cancelling appointments aren't really valid. They know they need to take care of their teeth, but they're putting it off. Something else has come up, and crossing you off their list seems the easiest thing to do. If you can offer them options *besides* cancelling, it makes things a bit less easy. That makes a surprisingly big difference: more often than not, people opt to do the right thing and keep the appointment as originally scheduled, if not earlier than originally scheduled.

The Ultimate Patient Arrival and Greeting

That successful first call brings Mrs. Adams to your office on Thursday afternoon. The first thing she should feel upon arrival is that your office space presents well; it's welcoming and clean. That means no scuff marks, no dirty windows, no dirty door handles, no crooked pictures, and no old signs. Everything that Mrs. Adams sees when she arrives should confirm her decision that your Dental Office is indeed the right Dental Office for her.

Practices that provide an Ultimate Patient Experience don't even have waiting rooms, as you'll recall. They have client lounges that are warm and welcoming. When Mrs. Adams enters that lounge, there's a small, clearly designated area that draws her to it on her arrival. If that area and the lounge are set up correctly, she simply follows the natural flow of the layout and goes over to be greeted.

When Mrs. Adams arrives at your office, the person who greets her already has a good idea who Mrs. Adams is. Everyone in your office has a copy of your appointment schedule, so everyone knows who should be arriving at two o'clock. Mrs. Adams is coming for a filling, Mr. Roberts is coming to see the hygienist, and Mrs. Miller is coming to have a permanent crown seated. Your greeter already knows Mr. Roberts and Mrs. Miller, so she can easily identify Mrs. Adams. She greets her with a smile and says, "Welcome to Dream Dental. You must be Mrs. Adams. I'm Jenny. I spoke with you on the phone." It's best to make sure that the team member who made Mrs. Adams' appointment can be there to greet her, if possible. But if that can't happen, then the greeter can say, "I'm Kate. I know Jenny made your appointment, because she told me so much about you. I've been looking forward to meeting you." This warm, concierge-class greeting continues the message to Mrs. Adams that Dream Dental offers World Class Customer Service.

Jenny gestures toward the lounge, saying, "Please make yourself comfortable. I'll go and let Dr. Moffet know that you're here."

She does not say, "Take a seat," and certainly not, "We'll be with you in a few minutes" or, "Won't be too long." If Mrs. Adams is the kind of client you want, she doesn't appreciate being treated brusquely or being told to wait any more than you do.

While Mrs. Adams begins to make herself comfortable, she rarely receives a clipboard of paperwork to complete. This is because any necessary forms and paperwork have been mailed or e-mailed to her well in advance of her visit. Otherwise, if Mrs. Adams arrives on time for a two o'clock appointment and has ten minutes of paperwork to complete, you can't possibly get her in for treatment until 2:10 p.m. or 2:15 p.m. That's 10 or 15 minutes eaten out of your day, and you want to avoid anything that creates such delays.

Now, if Mrs. Adams were to arrive early, that's something that could give you a leg-up timewise. You would want to recognize it in a positive way. Often, dental offices do just the opposite by saying to the patient, "Oh, you know you're early?" To the patient, that can sound like, "Are you stupid? Why are you here early?"

When Mrs. Adams arrives early, Jenny says, "Thanks so much for coming in early. Let me tell Dr. Moffet, because you never know, we may be able to see you ahead of time." Translation: "If you arrive early, we like that. Sometimes, we can see you early, and that really helps the flow of our day. We're going to go out of our way to show our appreciation." That's the law of reciprocity in action again, and it's another way in which solid relationships are built: you give me something, I give you something in return, and we both end up happy.

The Ultimate Handover

The smooth transfer of patient from client lounge to treatment room is the next step in creating the Ultimate Connection between your patient and your practice. It's a step that dentists typically miss because they tend to do transplants rather than transfers. Often what happens is a door off the waiting room opens, someone barks, "Mrs. Adams?" And when Mrs. Adams quickly dumps her magazine and stands up, she's simply told, "Follow me."

Here's how an Ultimate Patient Experience Handover works. True to her word, Jenny has gone back to tell Mary, the dental assistant, of Mrs. Adams' arrival. She also tells Mary precisely where Mrs. Adams is sitting in the client lounge. Because you work from a schematic that numbers all the seats, Jenny can easily say to Mary, "Mrs. Adams is here for her two o'clock appointment. She's sitting in seat three. She's wearing a red sweater, and she has long brown hair." When it's time to bring Mrs. Adams in for her appointment, Mary goes into the lounge, walks over to Mrs. Adams, and says, "Hello, Mrs. Adams. I'm Mary, and I'm going to be assisting Dr. Moffet today. How is your day going so far?'

It's critically important that Mary ask this kind of specific question, rather than "How are you doing?" or "How are you today?" A specific question evokes a specific response, and Mary is tuned in for anything about Mrs. Adams' day that could be different the next day. I call this Secret Service Information. I train teams to find little pieces of secret information that the patient can share with you and that you can share back to connect with her at another point in time.

Let's say Mrs. Adams answers, "My day's been okay, but it's going to get hectic. I'm hosting a dinner party tonight and have so much to do!" When Mrs. Adams comes in for her next appointment, Mary can say, "Oh, last time you were in, you told me that you'd been running around because you were having people over for dinner that night. How did that dinner party go?" Using Secret Service Information helps create an Ultimate Patient Experience for Mrs. Adams because it makes her think, "Wow! They remember me here. They really are interested in me."

For today's appointment, Mary replies, "It sounds like you've got an exciting evening ahead. Won't you please come with me?" And Mary transfers Mrs. Adams to the treatment room.

The transfer itself is efficient and quick, without conversation. This is because you cannot have a face-to-face conversation while you're walking down a corridor. The reason is because while you're both moving, you will miss out on getting that valuable visual feedback from the patient, and the patient misses out on getting valuable visual feedback from you. Conversation under such conditions is counterproductive because Mary can miss some really important Secret Service Information that she would have captured and been able to use later. So all Mary says to Mrs. Adams is, "All right, we're going down the hallway, around the corner to the right, into the first room on the left." She gives Mrs. Adams clear, specific instructions, and she lets Mrs. Adams lead the way, redirecting her if she starts making any wrong turns.

When Mrs. Adams enters the door of the treatment room, she may not know where she should put her handbag or where she's meant to sit. So Mary lets her know "You can pop your bag right here if you'd like." Mary also says "Make yourself comfortable" and motions toward the treatment chair.

That's the process of transfer. It ends when Mrs. Adams has her bib on and Mary sits down beside her, facing her, and resumes the conversation started in the lounge: "So, tell me about that dinner party that you're getting ready for."

The Dentist's Entrance

When you enter the room to treat your patient, the wheels of dentistry need to start spinning. You can't waste time waiting for a conversation to end. When Mary sees you enter, she ends her chat with Mrs. Adams by telling her, "Dr. Moffet is here now."

Then again, the wheels can't spin so fast that Mrs. Adams feels like nothing but a block of time out of your calendar. You greet her warmly, introduce yourself, and briefly go over the task ahead in a friendly way. "We're doing a filling on that upper tooth today. Let me get you numb first." If you need to exit because you're still working on another patient, you can say something like "Mrs. Adams, I'm going to get you started, and then I'm just finishing up something next door. Please excuse me. I'll be a few minutes while that's going numb." Mrs. Adams won't mind at all, because she knows her treatment is progressing. Plus, she has a pleasant conversation to get back to with Mary.

In The Ultimate Patient Experience, the dentist does three things: he greets the patient, he treats the patient, and then he bids the patient farewell. Other than that, every other duty needed should be performed by your team members.

A major exception to that general rule is that *you*, the dentist, are in charge of the dental chair.

When you go in to greet Mrs. Adams, and when you go back in to begin her treatment once she's numb, she's sitting up to converse with Mary. But when you put the chair back, that means you're ready to go, and when you put the chair up, you've either finished or you're leaving the room momentarily. Of course, putting Mrs. Adams in the right position for your magnifiers is important, so you politely ask, "Can you just slide up the chair a little for me, please, Mrs. Adams?" Or you say, "Thank you. You're perfect now." Once again, little compliments and a thank-you will always work a subtle magic. When Mrs. Adams does something for you, you want to let her know she's exceptional for doing it.

Pleasant conversation between you and Mrs. Adams can and should continue throughout the treatment process, albeit in a goal-oriented way. This is *your* time to build some rapport with Mrs. Adams, while still showing her that you are on top of her dental treatment needs. It's a time for you to be courteous, caring, and professional, all at the same time.

I know of offices where the dentist will chat with the dental assistant in the patient's presence about what they're doing over the weekend, what their family is up to, or how the kids are doing in school. In your dream practice, that's strictly forbidden. Your patient can never be made to think—"Hey, hello, I'm down here!" They can never be made to start to wonder if you've forgotten that they're actually there. The customer you've attracted expects, deserves, and must receive one hundred percent of your attention! Always!

At the other extreme, some practices can be so treatment focused and clinical they take the focus off their patients in another way. The dentist gets down to business, barking instructions at the dental assistant like Alan Alda shouting "Scalpel!" and "Suction!" on *M*A*S*H*. This does not help poor Mrs. Adams feel welcome or at ease. In fact, she's likely to feel you want her done and out of the way. Once again, the example you set speaks volumes, so you show Mrs. Adams you're a warm and caring person by taking the time to say, "Please," "Thank you," and "You're welcome" to your assistant each time you need to ask for something.

To communicate effectively with patients during treatment, I like to preface what I'm going to say with a gentle touch on their shoulder. It makes an extra connection and alerts their senses to what I'm about to say. I'll just place my hand lightly on their shoulder and ask, "How are you doing down there?" If Mrs. Adams is going to be treated for 30 minutes, it's nice for you to check in on her regularly and for her to be able to communicate back, even with a small nod and an "uh-huh" to let you know she's fine.

The Magic Post-It Note

Dale Carnegie wrote, "Remember that a man's name is to him the sweetest and most important sound in the language." And I couldn't agree more. Addressing your patients by using their name is vital in making and building a personal connection with them.

While you're actually treating your patient, however, you can easily become so focused on procedural detail, so engrossed in the process, that you momentarily forget your patient's name. We've all done it. You sit there over a Mrs. ... Mrs. ... Mrs. who? and you struggle to find wherever that name has gone within your brain.

In other businesses, remembering Mrs. Adams' name would be far easier than it is in the dental treatment room. Attorneys, accountants, and similar professionals have paperwork with their client's name on it right in front of them. All they have to do is glance at it to address the client correctly. But in the treatment room, the patients name is in small writing on a computer screen or a chart and sometimes on a chart or screen that's literally behind your own back.

The awkwardness of forgetting a patient's name is something I can't tolerate, so I developed a simple and practical, yet

Continued on next page

low-tech solution. Before bringing the patient down to the treatment room, the dental chairside assistant writes the patient's name in big letters on a yellow Post-it note and sticks that note on the edge of the bench in the treatment room. Once the patient is in the chair and I start the chair reclining, I simply take the Post-it note off the bench and stick it to the corner of the patient's dental bib.

Using a magic Post-it note puts my patient's name right there in front of me so I can read it anytime I need to. Best of all, my patient doesn't even know it's there. To make the Post-it note even more magical, I also have my assistant jot down the patient's next appointment date, and the reason for that appointment, on the bottom of the note. When I'm finished with today's procedure, I can simply lift the Post-it note off the bib as I put the chair back up to vertical and bid that patient a very courteous farewell: "Mrs. Adams, it's been great seeing you today. Good luck with that dinner party, and I'll see you for your hygiene visit in August. I think it's the 23rd?

Imagine how much you impress your patients when you can "remember" the details of their next appointments without clicking away at the computer screen for this information the way every other dentist does.

The Clear Next Step

Think back to the finest meal you ever enjoyed at a World Class restaurant. It wasn't just the food that was excellent; it was the *entire experience*. From the time you made your reservation, you were treated with respect and courtesy. Every minute you were there, each step was clear. You knew where your table was because you were smoothly escorted to it. You knew who your servers were because they identified themselves. If you needed the restroom you were always directed there with courtesy. These clear steps ensured you always felt valued. You never encountered unpleasant surprises or felt awkward or confused.

Unpleasant surprises, awkwardness, and confusion are serious Customer Service saboteurs. With that in mind, I've applied the principles of that World Class fine dining Experience to develop a Dental Customer Service philosophy I call the Clear Next Step. With the Clear Next Step, everything you do in your dental office is designed to leave your valued patients with total clarity about what their next step is to be. It's the reason the greeting area is easily identifiable, the reason team members offer clear instructions, and the reason smooth seamless handovers are exactly how they are. One of the most crucial applications of the Clear Next Step occurs when the handover of the patient from the Dentist back to the dental assistant takes place at the completion of treatment.

This handover cannot suffer because you're in a hurry to get to your next patient in another room or because Mary's in a hurry to get Mrs. Adams' room ready for its next use. Mrs. Adams still gets your undivided attention, just as you received the server's undivided attention in that restaurant. And just as the server gracefully cleared your table, stacking plates up one arm in a well rehearsed and efficient manner, the completion of treatment is well choreographed and well rehearsed.

You return Mrs. Adam's chair back to vertical while pushing the bracket table and tray away, so they're well clear of her and she cannot knock into them as she reorients herself. Mary, who's waiting attentively, hands Mrs. Adams a warm towel and a filled cup for rinsing. The top priority is *still* Mrs. Adams' comfort and well-being, not the instruments, not the tear down, not the next setup, and not the next patient.

Only after all this has transpired can you hand Mrs. Adams back to Mary. But just before you do, you need to tell Mrs. Adams the following five things:

1. **Tell her exactly what treatment she has received today:** how many fillings were completed, how many tooth surfaces were involved, how deep those fillings were, and if any changes were made to the expected treatment (such as an increase in filling size due to the presence of additional decay).

2. **Tell her exactly what she may experience or feel over the next few days.** This way, she's prepared for any and all symptoms that might occur after treatment. (Remember, no unhappy surprises.)

3. **Explain the exact treatment she will be having at her next visit to the dental office.**

4. **Let her know the time frame or urgency of the remaining treatment required.** Your role here is to create

urgency in Mrs. Adams' mind, as opposed to a lack of urgency. Even if that next visit is to see the hygienist, informing her of every exact need for that visit helps your front office team secure that appointment.

5. **Tell her exactly what will happen if her next treatment is not carried out.** This helps to establish the urgency mentioned above. Plus, it's your duty, as a dentist who provides quality care, to educate Mrs. Adams on the consequences of delaying or neglecting her prescribed treatment

Once you're confident that Mrs. Adams has a clear understanding of these five important points, you're back to personal connections. You thank her for her time, compliment her on being such a great patient for you that day, and recognize any significant event coming up for her between this visit and her next visit. For returning patients, this may be something you've discussed with them already or some Secret Service information your team has passed along to you. For Mrs. Adams, Mary will have cued you in when you first entered the treatment room: "We were just discussing a dinner party Mrs. Adams is having tonight." For a final "Wow factor," wish Mrs. Adams a wonderful party before you say farewell and depart.

World Class Front Office Follow-Up

If you've ever watched an Olympic relay, you know how wonderful it is to observe a perfect baton change. The runner in front never has to look back; he's running at pace with his hand reaching behind and really takes off when the baton is placed firmly in his hand. Then, it's his job to make sure that baton gets squarely into the hand of the next team member so that that runner can continue the relay. If the baton is dropped, or the handover is sloppy, the opportunity to win is gone. Bringing home the gold isn't about who's fastest; it's really about who passes the baton the best. You've just passed the baton back to Mary, so now *she's* in charge of winning the race.

Back in Mary's capable hands, Mrs. Adams is made comfortable, clean, and presentable. When she's ready, she's helped out of the dental chair, her handbag is passed to her, and she is walked to the front office. Ideally, once there, she's seated in a private area. It's not a stand or a counter; it's an area where there's no audience and also no distraction of people coming and going. Mary has related to Rita, the front office person to whom Mary's handing the baton, the five things you, the dentist, just told Mrs. Adams. Mrs. Adams gets to hear all this important information again, spoken clearly in lay terms, rather than jargon or technical terms, as well as in terms of the removal of pathology. This is a seemingly small point that can have a huge impact when it comes to your bottom line. This is because a lot of the general public can have an attitude toward dentistry that says, "My teeth don't hurt now, and the problem is fixed. So why should I worry anymore?" This attitude can often turn into the thought, "My teeth weren't hurting before, and they don't hurt now, either—but now I'm hurting in the wallet."

So Mary relays to Rita, "Dr. Moffet needs to remove some active decay on these teeth, a, b, and c, next time." She does not say, "Mrs. Adams needs three more fillings." Rita says to Mrs.

Adams, "Oh, so Dr. Moffet wants to remove active decay from three teeth next time?"

Rita has a mental checklist of all the information she needs to receive, so she doesn't really speak until Mary has finished telling her everything she needs to. She listens carefully to make sure that Mary is covering everything on the list. Otherwise, if Mary misses anything, Rita will have to keep Mrs. Adams waiting while she goes down the back to Mary to ask for the missing information. Which means the baton gets dropped. And since Mary has other work to do, which she'll have to stop doing to answer Rita, the baton has now been dropped twice. To prevent this, Rita listens carefully and then repeats the information to Mrs. Adams in front of Mary. Once both team members have established that all handoff bases have been covered, Rita says, "Thank you, Mary." That's Mary's cue to turn to Mrs. Adams one last time. "Mrs. Adams, it was great seeing you today. I really hope that dinner party goes well, and I'm really looking forward to hearing about it next time you're back in to see us." Then, Mary goes back to clean up the treatment room and get it ready to receive her next patient. She's doesn't stay on as a social distraction.

You may have noticed a bit of repetition here: The patient is hearing everything from the dentist and then hearing it again from the dental assistant, who's speaking to the person at the front office, who's repeating it back to the patient (all in an anything but parrot-like fashion, by the way). This repetition is more than necessary; it's absolutely vital. Each repetition is a checkpoint in the relay run by you and your team, a point where the baton can be smoothly and securely passed.

Passing the baton properly every time makes winning the gold a given. Mrs. Adams quickly concludes, "They *clearly* know what they're doing here, and they *clearly* care about me." Rita shows concern for Mrs. Adams and her visit by making sure that Mrs. Adams is feeling good about her visit.

The Ultimate Handover easily allows Rita to arrange Mrs. Adams' next appointment and, funnily enough, because of this process, Mrs. Adams will often have her credit card out ready and even handed over, almost as a matter of course. It's all part of a seamless process. It's an exchange between friends first and foremost. When Mrs. Adams is ready to go, Rita will thank her kindly yet again, escort her to the lounge or to the front door, wish her good luck with her dinner party, and bid her a lovely good-bye.

Then, Mrs. Adams is off to tend to that dinner party, where she'll talk about the wonderful experience she had that day at Dream Dental.

5

Trapped by Time and How to Break Free

In both my consulting business and my social circles, I hear constant complaints from dentists about time, or, more accurately, the lack of it. These dentists complain about schedules that are so jam-packed they can never take a break. They can't shorten their workday or workweek, and they can't even think of taking a vacation. They seem to bear their time burdens like some odd badge of honor. They play comparative games of "my time pressures are more brutal than yours" and try to one-up each other on how long they've gone without vacation days. "I didn't even take a vacation last year" is trumped by "Really? Well, I haven't taken a vacation in three years," and the most wretched case wins. Hearing such "comparathons" makes me feel wretched *for* these dentists. But if my old friend Philip could hear them, he'd only shake his head and laugh.

You see, Philip told me a story, years ago, that really stuck with me. He's always had a thriving practice and has loved to travel for pleasure, so much so that he and his wife decided to take a tour of Europe that lasted for three months. Here's what Philip did before taking his three-month leave from his practice. First, before he left, Philip approached seven neighboring dentists and asked if they could each, individually, look after any of his patients who might need treatment during a specific two-week period while he was away. That two-week "stand-by" period for emergency-care services would be allocated among each of the seven neighboring dentists. And with that arrangement in place for his patients, off he went.

When it came to looking at the financial impact that three months off had on Philip's practice, the results were astounding. In the year that Philip was absent for three months, his collections were pretty well exactly the same as they were in the previous year. They were also equal to what he collected in the following year, and in both of those years Philip worked the full twelve months! That's right. At the end of the financial year in which he took the twelve-week leave, he'd made exactly the same income in nine months that he'd made the previous year, working twelve full months, and that he made the following year, also working twelve full months.

Philip's experience illustrates an aspect of the familiar truism "Time is Money", which is missed by dentists who don't know the secret of World Class Customer Service. While time is indeed money, there are smart ways to handle time so it enhances customer satisfaction, letting you work *fewer* hours while boosting your bottom line.

The Time Trap of Missed Vacations

Dentists who never take a vacation because they think their patients need them too much aren't viewing the situation through Customer Service Eyes. As a good friend once said to me, "If you were the patient, who would you want to have treating your teeth: a dentist who *takes* a vacation or a dentist who *needs* a vacation?" With this in mind, you don't just *deserve* to take time off; you *need* to take time off. You need it more than your patients actually need you, and my friend Philip can prove it.

First and foremost, Philip had a practice full of clients he'd provided with quality, caring service for years. In fact, that's the chief reason he was able to afford his fabulous vacation. So here's how Philip did it.

He allocated staff to work in his office purely for the purpose of taking calls. If any of Philip's patients got into difficulty and needed to see a dentist urgently, the phone staff knew to refer them to the dentist on standby that week.

Patient calls were handled in a well thought out way:

"Are you in any pain or discomfort?"

"No, not really."

"Are you happy to wait until Dr. Philip returns? He'll be back on this date, and I can make an appointment on this date. And if you get into any trouble, if it starts to hurt, just give me a phone call straightaway because I can get you in somewhere else immediately."

Callers didn't reach an answering machine telling them that the office was closed or that Philip would be back in three months. Phone staff didn't say, "He's not here. Call somewhere else," or "Dr. So-and-So is covering for him. Let me get you in to see him."

Because of the outstanding relationship Philip had built with his patients, and the outstanding procedures he had put in place, the overwhelming majority of his patients waited. Even those who needed urgent emergency treatment came right back to see Philip once he was home. None of his patients switched to his competitors' practices—not a single one.

The Time Trap of False Pressure

In your dream practice, patients can't feel lined up and in a hurry. A busy office shouldn't appear outwardly busy. The image you want to create for your customers is that of a swan gliding across the water. Underneath the water, the swan is busy paddling. On top of the water, it's all grace and charm. Time pressures spoil that entirely. People running about in stressed-out confusion evoke an image that's much closer to a flock of quacking, flapping ducks. Luckily, smart scheduling to eliminate this stress can reestablish an order that's graceful and pleasant for all involved.

An all-too-common way that Dentists create scheduling stress stems from the false sense of urgency they develop. Most dentists think that when they carry out treatments requiring multiple appointments, they need to get the patients right back in as quickly as possible. Let's use crown and bridge appointments as an example. Dentists who feel the time between taking the impression and placing the permanent crown needs to be as short as possible will tell the patient they can do it in one to two weeks, depending on their lab's turnaround time. This rush job puts undue pressure on your practice. You've got to immediately find time in the appointment book to get the patient in on the rushed schedule that you have just created. And if there's even a slight delay at the lab, then you've got to reschedule the patient and again find time in the appointment book.

Now, let's look at what happens if you tell patients at their initial appointment that the wait time for the crown will be three weeks. You gain so much flexibility. If the crown arrives back a day or two later than the usual two weeks, you've still got plenty of time up your sleeve. And if you ask patients when they leave after their initial appointment, "If your crown arrives back sooner, would you like us to call you?" things get even better. You look like a hero because you're working to make things happen. Those patients are ready to jump for you, instead of you having to jump for them if something at the lab causes an unexpected holdup or delay.

I've had plenty of dentists tell me, "My patients won't wait three weeks for a crown!" My reply is, "It's not really a discussion topic at the dinner table, is it?" Seriously, when was the last time you actually heard someone say, "Your dentist makes you wait three weeks for a crown? That's horrid. You should never put up with waiting more than two." Patients just don't do that. Granted, there are dental offices that do have the ability to make their crowns onsite, and they offer that as a value-added service to the patient. At least, that's how I believe they should offer it. For the clients you're attracting, the clients you want, knowing they're getting a quality product will trump instant results every time. When patients are assured of quality and value, they will wait, in the same way Philip's patients waited for him to return from touring Europe.

Since I used crowns as the example here, I'll add another word on quality. To earn you a saner schedule, the quality of your temporary crowns has to be, literally, rock solid. If it's not, you've got a problem that can't be fixed. More than half of the temporary crowns I place have to be drilled off. They're not going to come off on their own before that permanent crown is placed. Temporary crowns that regularly come off early are usually the result of shoddy work that would definitely be talked about at the dinner table.

The Time Trap of Shoddy Dentistry

My consultancy business takes me literally all around the world. In addition, I take a few weeks' vacation each year. And when I'm in the dental office, I'm there seeing patients only three days a week. My schedule leads a lot of people to ask, "How can you possibly be away from your practice so often and for so long?" My answer is threefold:

1. I have wonderful patients whom I value and who value me.
2. I have excellent systems and procedures in place to tend to those patients.
3. I don't do shoddy dentistry.

Making sure that your work is good enough to stand the test of time takes enormous time pressure off you. I treat my patients comprehensively. Their teeth are fixed so they don't fail or break. This frees up valuable time in my practice, since my team and I aren't constantly surprised with calls from patients who say, "You know that filling you did two months ago? It's broken. You've got to get me in straightaway so you can fix it."

Continued on next page

Dentists who do shoddy dentistry get caught in ever-growing time traps. They patch mouths up and those patches fail, so patients need to be seen frequently and immediately. If you do solid work instead of patch-up jobs, you're giving your patients a better product. It not only lasts longer but the patient who's got it will wait longer to see you rather than going elsewhere.

The Time Trap of Fees That Are Too Low

Dentists get trapped by time all the time for the simple reason that they don't schedule regular fee increases. They just keep on working for the same fee, while inflation and time eat away at their bottom line. Staff members want raises, rent goes up, and lab fees and material costs increase. The only way most dentists know to increase their collections and meet these demands is to work faster, work longer, and take less time off. Before they know it, they're caught in a vortex: they can't take time off to go to a seminar, see their child play soccer, or star in a play, and they certainly can't take a vacation. They might not even be able to afford to. Their longer hours are only keeping them from going under. They're certainly not increasing profits.

In 2002 I received some life changing advice about fees. I was attending a newly formed dentist mastermind group, and the facilitator told us we should all return to our offices and put our fees up. Interestingly, I'd just put mine up by 5 percent. But our facilitator told me that 5 percent was not enough. So I went back to my office and immediately put my fees up another 5 percent, which meant I'd increased them by a total of 10 percent in a matter of only a few short months.

Guess what? Nothing happened, by which I mean nothing happened besides a healthy increase in my profits. I didn't lose a single patient. Not one person complained. Twelve months later, I put my fees up another 10 percent. And the next year, I put them up *another* 10 percent. And I still didn't receive a single complaint or question about my fee levels.

I'll admit to feeling a little guilty at that point. So, for the next three years following that, I put my fees up by 6 percent annually. No patients were lost; no one complained. Then I started feeling guilty again and developed a schedule I could live with, putting my fees up by 3 percent every six months for the next two years.

No one *ever* complained. My patients never even noticed.

Think about it. People take their cars to the mechanic and get three things fixed. Then, two years later, the mechanic has to fix those two or three things again. Customers of an auto repair service don't say, "Oh, the price on this or that is 10 percent higher than it was two years ago." If they notice a difference, they write it off to increases in materials and labor.

On the flip side, utility customers do notice when the price of electricity goes up, because they're getting that bill on a regular basis. They say, "Wait! It's still the same electricity as it was six months ago. Why am I having to pay more?" That's why I recommend quarantining your hygiene fees if you can. Patients will notice even a slight fee increase every six months if they're dutifully and regularly coming in for the same service. Costs to your practice for hygiene treatment don't increase substantially anyway, so it's not going to damage your bottom line if you keep those fees steady.

Once I was comfortable with where my fees were, it was irrelevant what my neighbors were charging. I just kept putting my fees up, based on inflation and time. I didn't check what my neighbors were charging for this and that. I didn't need to as long as I had satisfied patients who were happy to pay what I was charging. As a result, the fee for a crown in my office is dramatically higher than that of neighboring dentists. Yet half of my income comes from people having crowns, which are easily quantifiable from one office to another. People can just call around and ask, "How much is a crown here, how much is a crown there?" In my office, patients know that the reason they pay that higher fee is because they get exceptional quality and service from me.

If you're focused on World Class Customer Service and you're giving your patients an Ultimate Patient Experience, then you're attracting the clients you want and you're taking excellent care of them. These clients aren't going to ditch you over an annual fee increase. Dentists who don't increase their fees regularly are depriving themselves of money and time. They're depriving themselves of freedom.

The Time Trap of Stacking Your Book

I know some dental consultants who teach their clients to "stack" their appointment book. This means that the first appointment is scheduled at whatever time the office opens, then the next one goes on top of that and the next one goes on top of that. I'm actually quite horrified when I hear consultants say they advise dentists to do this. The idea is that if everything goes as planned, you get to go home early. When it comes to time management in your office, nothing's a bigger recipe for disaster.

The funny thing about those consultants is that they often aren't dentists themselves.

I guess if all those "stacked" patients show up on time, if you don't encounter any unanticipated disruptions to your day, and if you haven't got enough patients, stacking appointments will get you home early. But even under those impossible conditions, stacking's promise to get you home early will backfire. The people on your team who are paid by the hour won't be getting a full paycheck, which means they won't stick with you for long. Plus, all the small but critical things that need to be done during each staff member's downtime *don't* get done because of the way stacking compresses the appointment book.

Stacking your appointment schedule the way those consultants advise you to is pure madness. It's not even structured, and lack of structure causes Dental Offices to falter, if not totally collapse, on a daily basis. At best, stacking creates disorder. At worst, it wreaks sheer havoc on your practice and your team.

Luckily, I know a better way, a much better way. I teach clients to work their books backward and to template what I call the Ultimate Appointment Book.

The Ultimate Appointment Book is perfect for giving your day the following:

- **Flow.** Knowing what type of appointment needs to go where ensures the swan is gliding smoothly across the water. It establishes a steady stream of patients and duties throughout the day

- **Financial security.** Ultimate Appointment Books ensure that sufficient income is earned by the Dental Office for each week. They eliminate those days, weeks, and even months of frantic "busyness" that still don't yield enough profits to pay the bills. This is, perhaps, the greatest of its gifts. Nothing is more draining than a day jam-packed with short appointments backed up on top of each other and then getting to the end of the day and finding out that you haven't even covered your wages and salaries. Stack several of these days back to back, and you're an emotional mess as well as a financial mess

- **Balance.** A balanced appointment book has a comfortable mix of pleasant procedures and is not weighted unfavorably in any direction. The hygiene day contains appropriately placed maintenance appointments, perio-only appointments, and new patient appointments. The dentist's day isn't overweighted with short, 15-minute consultations, nor does it contain a predominance of crown and bridge seatings.

- **Coordination.** A well thought out appointment book safeguards against unintentional logjams created by careless or thoughtless scheduling. For example, root canal therapy and other procedures involving rubber dam won't be scheduled at times when the dentist must leave the patient for hygiene checks in other rooms. And hygiene checks aren't scheduled to be in conflict with long, new-patient consultations or implant procedures. Basically, the rules of common sense reign.

How do you create a book that accomplishes all of this? Well, you stack it. But you stack it far differently from the way unwise dental consultants advise you to stack it. You stack it correctly and systematically. You stack it just as I learned to stack the woodpile down at my farm.

Last spring, the manager of our small farm in Burrawang, New South Wales, gathered a bunch of fallen tree trunks, chopped them up, and left them for collection in different paddocks on the property. My family and I were at the farm for Christmas, and our manager went off to visit *his* family. As he did so, his parting words to me were, "If you've got nothing to do, you could always bring up the wood from the paddocks."

What a joker!

Unfortunately (or, perhaps, fortunately), a lot of that chopped wood was visible from our kitchen window. All through the holiday, it served as a daily reminder of my manager's parting jibe to me. And one day, I did have nothing to do. So I got into my truck, drove across the property, and hauled what turned out to be quite a considerable amount of wood up to my woodshed. Being the dental consultant I am, I started to think about maximizing efficiency as I tackled all that chopped wood. And the woodpile in my shed became a metaphor for the perfect dental appointment book.

You see, the woodpile needed to be well stocked and well stacked in neat rows. Well stocked, well stacked, wide and deep. And so I got to thinking. You see, the two big loads of wood in the paddocks from which I had to make the woodpile became a metaphor for the general population, all the people who come to a dental practice.

The first load of wood contained lighter colored wood, chopped fairly evenly and consistently, that was easy to gather, easy to pack on my truck, and easier to sort. The second load of wood was different. With more wood than the first, it was less evenly chopped and contained a lot of twisted pieces. It actually took more trips to move it and much more time to sort.

Back at the shed, stacking the pieces to construct my woodpile became a science. Some pieces were heavy and solid, while others were lighter. Some pieces were square and regular while others were curved and irregular. Stacking the woodpile so it didn't topple over, so that the rows were even and orderly, and the entire construction was secure took physical effort. Just as importantly, it took some thought.

Here's how to apply the lessons from the woodpile to optimize time and profitability in your appointment book:

1. Know how many woodpiles you need. Determine your financial goal for the year based on practice expenses, practice maintenance and improvement, salaries of doctors and team, and return on investment. This is your big number. Now figure the number of days your office will be open for the year: 365 minus holidays, weekends, and vacations. You'll want to build in a few days for things such as seminars, school functions, and emergency time away.

2. To arrive at the number of woodpiles you need, which, metaphorically speaking, are your daily production goals, divide your big number by the number of working days in your year.

3. Now that you know how many woodpiles you'll be stacking, use them to establish an ultra-efficient workweek. A well-stocked woodpile needs a strong foundation, so build it with foundational appointments; those high-production appointments such as crowns and implants that contribute the most to your daily production goal. For every day you work, organise those productive appointments in your book first.

   Stand back for a moment and take a look. Say you've worked out that you want to collect $10,000.00 a day, and your high-production appointments are crowns. You can get two-thirds of your daily income met by doing three crown appointments in a day, so you place those crown appointments strategically in your book. You may want to begin the day with one, pop another one in prior to lunch, as well as after lunch, and then end your day with another. Voila! The most important contributors to your bottom line are already in there.

4. Stack the lighter pieces on top of your foundation. These are the shorter appointments that come in second on your profitability list. Treatments such as fillings and orthodontics get booked in around your foundational appointments. The smallest pieces, such as dentures and consultations get stacked on the top of your now secure pile.

Templating your book in this "woodpile" way ensures that you never end up with a nickel-and-dime day of less profitable work. Let's run some numbers. If you're doing an eight-hour day, and you've got three crown appointments each day in which you're drilling a crown, you'll also need three shorter appointments to seat those new crowns. That makes four and a half hours of crown and bridgework out of an eight-hour day. That only leaves you with three and a half hours of schedule to fill with fillings and orthodontics.

A day like this is more productive for you, for your staff, and for your patients. You already know how a day filled with nothing but short appointments wears you out. Well, it wears everybody else out too. It keeps everyone in your office jumping from task to task without a break, which is exhausting. And it wears your patients out. Instead of looking like a graceful swan, your practice appears to be a bunch of ducks swimming around in circles.

One caution about woodpiles: On different days, the world out there will provide you with different loads to stack. Sometimes, the wood will be chopped neatly, so it's easy to stack from the bottom up. On other days it will be more complex and varied. You'll get handed some crazily shaped pieces of wood. You might even find a snake in the woodpile, a cancellation that needs to be filled, a late patient arrival, or a new or existing patient who needs some relief from pain and must be worked into your schedule. They can throw you a bit off balance. If your goal is to collect $10,000.00 each day, you can't always guarantee the pile will come in that way. What you can do is always work *toward* balance. Every doctor hates having a day when he makes $2,000.00, followed by a day he makes $13,000.00. If you build your woodpiles from the foundation up, you'll avoid that. Though you may not hit a perfect ten each and every day, you'll always achieve the sanest, most profitable weekly balance possible.

Know Your Numbers

Time and money are inseparable assessment factors in business. Everything you do to one factor impacts the other (and of course, your bottom line). That means to spot time traps, or for that matter, *any* weaknesses in processes and systems, you have to know what your practice's numbers are. You've got to know your numbers. That's an absolute no-brainer. I'm constantly floored by the number of dentists who call me and just don't know all their crucial numbers. You may know yours already. If so, that's great. But, just in case, here's a handy list of the numbers you need to know.

- collections and production, daily, weekly, and monthly.
- new patient inquiries
- where each prospective customer found out about your practice
- conversion numbers: how many prospects that call your office become new patients and collating these to each source of marketing and advertising
- appointments being rescheduled
- appointments being cancelled and not rescheduled
- new patients who cancel their appointment or simply fail to show up

Counting Crowns

A good rule of thumb for high-production appointments such as crowns and implants is to track them to make sure the same number come in as go out. By this I mean that if you cut three crowns on one day, you also want to seat three crowns that same day.

You don't ever want to find yourself with a day in which you're seating six and preparing none, because, ideally, you're billing for crowns at the time you cut them. So, if you seat six, and it takes half an hour to do each, you're doing three hours of work you've already been paid for. Your ledger is going to show that today you've now done three hours of no-fee work. If you seat three and drill three, however, your ledger is as balanced as your appointment books. It builds consistency into your schedule and your bottom line.

Freeing up time, once you get trapped, takes good timing in itself. You can't just turn up one day and say, "Starting tomorrow, we're going to be moving people around to make the book look better." What you must do is pick a date when the book is either empty or only 20 percent full and say, "This is the date when our new templating is going to start."

The front office team may object to this change if new templating isn't done at the right time in the development of your Ultimate Patient Experience focus. Without proper training in phone and communication skills, for example, they'll react by saying, "Oh, that person will never come in at that time.

This person will never agree to coming in at this time." But when introduced as part of the total process that I guide my clients through, these problems are minimal. I've helped many clients use the book templating, fee schedules, and other techniques I teach to break free from time traps and become far more productive and profitable, in as little as four to eight weeks.

Smart Money (or Beware of Shiny Objects)

I recently spoke to a prospective client who was fascinated by "the next big thing." He came to me with what he thought was the perfect mindset: he'd improved on his practice constantly over the years, he said, but couldn't boost his profits any longer. The thing is, as I spoke to him, I learned that most of his so-called improvements had nothing to do with his patients. He'd renovated the same space twice, once to expand it. Fair enough. Renovations for more rooms and more equipment are easily justifiable; their benefits are demonstrable. But his second renovation was just change for change's sake, with one exception. He now had a room in which to stash all the fancy equipment he'd bought but later abandoned, all those big shiny objects he'd invested in but never really used.

Dentists are easily lured into purchasing big shiny objects. Dental technology is advancing at an admirable pace, and it's hard not to be impressed by the latest big thing. But unless you're going to put anything and everything you invest in to profitable use, it won't add anything to your bottom line. On the contrary, it will create debt and eat away at profits.

Shiny? Yes. Smart? Not Always.

Not too long ago, slick marketers told dentists that they'd be able to fill teeth with lasers. Patients wouldn't need needles and dentists would have these huge crowds of patients coming to their doors because they'd heard the dentists had lasers and didn't use needles or drills anymore. So a number of dentists bought these lasers, which did, indeed, remove decay from teeth. The trouble was the lasers were so darned slow that the advantage of *not* using a needle was lost. Patients wouldn't put up with the slowness. Plus, the number of people a dentist could see and the number of cavities a dentist could fill were dramatically reduced because of all the time the laser took. Most of the dentists who bought those lasers ended up switching back to the high-speed drill. As it turns out, the high-speed drill still does a heck of a lot of things well and efficiently compared to the laser.

To keep from serving as a very expensive dust collector, technology has to be chosen carefully, with your patients' and your own preferences in mind. A dentist I recently befriended at a conference ran into the latter type of trouble when he purchased a CAD/CAM machine without considering his own preferences carefully enough. He spent $165,000.00 so he could save $200 to $300 per tooth on lab costs. He didn't have a problem with the lab he'd used; he just thought he'd keep up with technology while saving himself some money. Unfortunately, he found that the amount of technical work it took to use the machine took him away from working with his patients. He also hadn't considered the cost of constantly updating the machine's software, which made the machine more expensive than he'd anticipated. "I know doctors who have these things and love them," he told me. "But I can't wait to be rid of it. As soon as it pays for itself, it's *gone*."

My new friend illustrates an important qualifier: dentists differ widely in the methods and technology they prefer and sometimes use technologies that are not really required in their practices. But as a good rule of thumb, it's best to look before leaping.

An even better rule of thumb is that the wisest investments for your dream practice are those that put Customer Service first.

My "Smart" Technology

One of the best investments I've made for my practice is having two large screen LED television monitors installed in each of my treatment rooms. One monitor is installed flat on the ceiling, over the patient's chair, so the patient can easily view it during treatment. A second monitor is mounted on the wall at the end of the dental chair. This one is also easily viewed by patients when they are seated in the dental chair. Both monitors can relay input from the treatment room computer and therefore have the ability to demonstrate to the patient anything that I might be doing. Patients never have to move their heads, necks, or bodies to see one of these monitors clearly. When I'm not using this system to educate patients, the overhead screen can play movies or regular television to enhance patients' experience during treatment.

Continued on next page

The return on the investment I have made in these monitors has been dramatic. Patients view them as an indication of a progressive and innovative dental office, so it enhances my practice's image. And the investment itself was inexpensive, very much so, compared to other shiny objects.

Smart Staff Size

If you've read this far, you've already learned dozens of smart money strategies. Developing World Class Customer Service and delivering an Ultimate Patient Experience is a smart money strategy in itself, and every step in the process is devoted to it. After all, what could be smarter than improving your bottom line while increasing your happiness and that of others? But there are some smart investments that we haven't yet covered. One is looking at the size of your Dental Team.

Plenty of dental consultants will lecture you about the dangers of a team that's too large. One of the first things they trumpet is the need to eliminate staff "bloat." I give my clients a bit more credit. The type of dentists that I deal with typically don't pay wages for people they don't need. My experience is that when you assess your practice with Customer Service Eyes, you're more likely to find that your team is too *small.*

The other day I was on an online dental forum where someone asked the question, "Who should answer the phone when the person who's supposed to answer it is busy with a live patient right in front of them?"

I typed, "We like to make sure that everybody has the ability to do everything well in our office. So, dental assistants can answer the phone, or our hygienists can answer the phone."

He typed back, "They're too busy. My office manager is too. Those are the only people I've got."

My forum friend had just answered his own question. If you find that people are simply juggling too many jobs to do one of them right, the only way to keep balls from getting dropped is to hire additional people.

Before you bristle and tell me that you didn't pick up this book to shell over additional salaries for staff, I'll tell you outright that I know only too well that many dentists dismiss the idea out of hand. I'll also advise that you not be "that dentist." When you put things down on paper, those extra salaries pay off handsomely.

Figure that an extra team member up front might cost you $20.00–$25.00 an hour. Are you going to book more than $20.00–$25.00 an hour of dental treatment during that hour by having that person there? The answer is yes, absolutely! What's that you say? Your phone calls don't really go unanswered that often? All right, but how do you know that one of the four calls you're missing every week (and I'm being very kind in my estimate here) isn't from someone who wanted a smile makeover? If you nail two or three of those calls by having a well-trained person ready to answer them, that well-trained employee has now paid for their own salary for the year and then some. That "and then some" means you just made smart money.

Remember Rachel, the client who called me because she knew she needed help and wanted a consultant who really knew dentistry? Seven months into our coaching relationship, I called her to find out how well The Ultimate Patient Experience was working to turn her practice into a more successful, more profitable one. When our discussion turned to collections, I asked her, "How'd you do last month?" She said, "Let me check. I think we collected $108,000.00." In fact, her collections had been $108,000, $103,000, $120,000, and $102,000, for the past four months. When she hired me seven months earlier, she was averaging only $60,000.00 per month. Things had certainly changed.

Rachel's accountant said to her, "Whatever you've been doing the last four months, just keep doing that." Well, Rachel hasn't done any extra marketing. She hasn't even increased her fees. What she's done is utilize the procedures and processes that I advise to train her team—including the new team member she hired four months ago—in The Ultimate Patient Experience.

Smart Marketing

Rachel's experience reveals another beauty of offering World Class Customer Service: If you put your focus on that singular secret, you don't need to worry about fancy marketing. You'll get the patients you want and need through word of mouth. And you'll keep them in your practice much longer, simply because patients who receive an Ultimate Patient Experience just don't leave.

Retaining patients is hugely important, as another peek at Rachel's success story reveals. When we first started looking at her numbers, she had a good supply of new patients, but she couldn't tell me how many prospective patients scheduled appointments that they then cancelled and did not reschedule. Nor could she tell me how many existing patients scheduled appointments, cancelled them, and didn't reschedule. When we added those numbers together, the total worked out to be equal to about one quarter of the number of new patients making appointments each month. That meant that twenty-five percent of her new patients were there simply to replace the patients who were cancelling and not rebooking

It also meant Rachel had a big money drain, one that stopped as soon as she took steps to stop those cancellations. Every time you can stop a patient cancelling, it's another patient you've kept. It's also a patient you now don't need to attract through additional marketing.

So many dentists just don't get that. They think, "I'll just up my ads and get more people in." I'm horrified when I hear dentists say, "My marketing is so successful that we see sixty new patients a month." My first thought is that these dentists should quit marketing and start rebooking. They should spend more time on their existing patients and turn them into evangelists for their dental practices. They should stop the leaks. If they don't, it's like putting a fire hose into a leaky barrel. They're sending tons of water in, but it's flooding out through gaps and cracks in their Customer Service systems.

The Smart Looking Website

Unless you've got top-notch skills in electronic media, investing in a top-quality website for your practice is smart money. My consultancy has a feature that lets dentists send me a form to book a strategy session with me. They send in the form, and I contact them for an interview to determine whether or not I can be their coach. Of course, I do my homework on each applicant before I get back to them, but, unbelievably, in some cases, I can't even find some of these dentists' websites. They don't have them. In other cases, I do find their websites, but their websites look like something worked up from a template some kid was given at the local high school.

In times past, patients came to your dental practice because they walked past your building, saw your brass plaque, and thought. "Well, that's a lovely plaque. And he's got a nice name." Later, they looked in the phone book. In this millennium, they head to the Internet and do their homework. This means you need a professional website that answers prospective patients' questions and personalizes your practice. You want a website that looks just as classy and just as interactive as a news website. It should not look as if it's been up there for years. It should be vibrant. It should have some of the latest dental news but not at the expense of its purpose, which is to make the prospective patient pick up the phone and make an appointment with you.

Never forget that The Ultimate Patient Experience is about making people feel welcome and connected. Let your website welcome them and connect to them with friendly images of your actual team (not stock photos). Consider sharing a little personal information about team members as well with simple profiles, such as "Kathy's been a dental hygienist for thirty years. She's been a valued member of our team for eight years. She loves baking biscuits." Now that you've got Customer Service Eyes, you can read between the lines to appreciate the power of something as simple as this.

These days a fair number of people don't just want to find you on the web; they want to connect with you. Facebook has become synonymous with connecting. Since The Ultimate Patient Experience involves making as many well thought out connections as you can with your patients, you need to have a proper Facebook presence. By *proper* I don't mean *stilted.* In fact, your practice's Facebook page needs to be far more conversational than your website. After all, Facebook is about friends.

All your Facebook postings should send a message that's both professional and friendly. Think upscale cocktail party—"Oh, you're an interesting person. What do you do for a living?"—not "I'm a dentist. You should come to me." Share reader-friendly dental news stories. They add to your reputation by showing patients you're in the dentistry loop and keeping current with things. You should also post things that you would share with friends in a social setting. These might include general interest topics such as "Nine Apps You Have to Have on Your Phone" and even recipes. Steer clear of scary news and anything political. You're here to connect, not debate.

Of course, your practice's Facebook page should feature your practice too but not in an ad-like way. I recently bought big foam gloves that look like the Facebook thumbs-up symbol. We now take photos of our team and patients wearing them and post them on our Facebook page. Patients love this idea. It's warm, friendly, and a lot of fun.

The moral of the story, when it comes to smart money, is that it's not always the biggest, flashiest things that give the best returns. And when it comes to creating an Ultimate Patient Experience, it's often the little things you do that matter the most.

Smart Space: The Two Treatment Room Practice

Occasionally, I consult with clients who have a single treatment room in their practice. One of the first questions I ask them is if they can possibly make room for another treatment room. I call that extra treatment room the great maximizer because of what it does for your day and for your practice's bottom line. A friend who has a practice not too far from my farm followed my advice and went from one treatment room to two, and it resulted in a major quantum leap for his practice.

I found out when I bought my first office that having only one treatment room robs you of ten minutes of time while tearing down and setting up between each and every patient appointment. You can't do anything but wait until that room is cleaned and set back up. Depending on how many daily appointments you have, you can lose more than two hours of valuable treating time every day. On top of that, a one treatment room office robs you of a critical component of The Ultimate Patient Experience: In a two room system the dental assistant can connect with the patient through friendly conversation while waiting for the dentist and then resume that connection when the dentist leaves the room. The relationship that this establishes is a great multiplier of income. It takes away that production line feeling you get when you use only one treatment room

Another disadvantage of the one room practice is that the dental assistant who treated the patient really just dumps the patient back out at the front desk. There's going to be no handover out there, because the assistant has got to go back and clean up the treatment room for the next patient. That next patient who's out there waiting is already watching all this going on and wondering, "Well, the dentist is finished with that patient. What's wrong with these people? Why can't I get in straightaway?" Patients don't understand that a room has to be stripped down, cleaned, sterilized, and set back up. They often only know that they're waiting, and they become impatient.

Expanding from one room to two rooms eliminates all these negatives. You can zigzag your way down your appointment book, which reduces your downtime substantially. But most importantly, you optimize the Customer Service Experience to maximize your bottom line. In fact, you'll recoup the full cost of setting up an additional treatment room within six months and reap pure profits from that point on.

Discounts Aren't Smart

A lot of dentists just give money away by telling patients, "Oh, I'll give you a discount for this, give you a discount for that," without ever totaling up what their discounts are actually costing them on a monthly basis. They're giving those discounts

Continued on next page

just to be a nice guy, but when I get the dentists to take a look at those numbers, they're shocked. "Gee, I've given away a semester's worth of my child's school fees this month," or "I've given away my monthly retirement investment." I advise against giving money away, especially if you don't know how much you're giving. When you're giving your patients an Ultimate Patient Experience, you're being the nicest guy there is. You don't need to give discounts. If you choose to do so, you need to keep a very close eye on how much you're giving away.

The Perfect Practice: Practice Makes Perfect

World Class athletes aren't born; they're made. Granted, some individuals are born with physical advantages that make them better at athletics than the average person. But there are plenty of others who rise to World Class status despite being born with athletic abilities that are average. Their athletic gifts may not be as great as those of others, yet they bypass the pack. They do so because they're dedicated. They practice. That's how they rise to the top. It's also how they stay there.

You may have gathered by now that I'm a bit of a sports fan. I'm particularly fond of golf. The World Class tour professional golfer is a fascinating example of how important practice is. To make a million or two dollars annually, tour pros practice about eight hours a day. They spend a considerable amount of that time practicing their swings.

One of the major reasons, if not *the* major reason, you picked up this book in the first place is that you thought your practice would be doing better by now than it actually is. Well, one would think that after years of playing, golf pros would have excellent swings. But for World Class golfers, excellence is an ongoing process. To keep winning, to stay on top, they keep revisiting their excellent swings through practice, practice, and more practice.

A truly successful dental practice is exactly the same. To achieve the success you really deserve, you've got to practice constantly. And to stay on top, you've got to practice some more. Providing consistent Ultimate Patient Experiences lifts your practice to higher levels of income and excellence, but it's an ongoing process. There's always something to fine tune, always some way to do things better. And while you're fine tuning your Ultimate Patient Experience, you need to constantly check back to make sure that the foundational things are still rock solid. Just as the professional golfer practices that swing to get to the top and stay there, you and your team have to practice Customer Service skills in order to achieve and maintain your Customer Service at a World Class level.

Mystery Shopping and Role Play

The ways in which you practice dentistry vary according to the skills you're accessing and developing. Again, I could probably write a book on practice techniques alone. But one of my favorite ways to put your front office through a few practice paces is the process of mystery shopping.

Mystery shopping is a nice way of saying, "spying to gather and analyze useful information." It involves creating a pretend customer to check out your business, and it's used regularly in all sorts of businesses. It's often used to check out competitors. In fact, your competitors may have already mystery shopped you. Mystery shopping is just as useful, if not more so, when used by businesses to assess themselves and determine how well procedures are being followed.

Practicality does limit the use of this technique in dentistry, since it can be tough to get a volunteer to mystery shop root canal or restorative procedures. Still, mystery shopping's ability to assess Customer Service makes it incredibly useful for checking the vital procedures performed in your front office.

This kind of mystery shopping is simple to do. Basically, all you need is a volunteer to make a call to your office and a way for you to listen in to the call. You also need a little bit of common sense. You probably have caller ID in your office, so having your wife call from home while you use the kitchen extension to listen in probably isn't the wisest way to go. Get a friend to help you, and listen in on that person's iPhone if you must. No one who answers calls these days gives a second thought to smartphones set on speaker. Your volunteer, posing as a prospective patient, simply phones your office, asks the typical questions a prospective patient asks, and gives your front office staff the information they need to put into the computer to make that appointment. You listen in during the call to assess whether all steps and stages of the process are being covered and performed at an optimal level.

I've actually mystery shopped my own front office (which, dare I say, performed to an exceptional level), so I know it can be a little unnerving to listen to your own team when you put them under the microscope. Suggesting to your team members improvements based on the results of mystery shopping can also take a little getting used to. But as with all things, it gets easier with practice. And because the information it provides improves the performance of your front office team, a little discomfort on your part and theirs is well worth the effort.

Another practice method that I can't recommend highly enough is role play. Clients who hire me really experience a remarkable improvement in results when the staff answering the phone regularly set aside time to role play various scenarios. The reason for this, of course, is that practice makes perfect and role play is practice in its truest sense. You're familiar with the concept: two people switch roles and perform them in a play-acting way. But the role play technique I teach, which I learned from a good friend of mine who's an expert in sales, is typically done in threes: One person plays the caller, the second plays the answerer, and the third is an observer. They then rotate the three roles and repeat. And then they do it again. This way each team member involved has the opportunity to experience all three roles.

The person who really learns the most during each of these role plays is the observer, since that team member gets to see both sides of the process occurring at the same time. Those who are focused on playing the caller or answerer are focused purely on that role. But observers can see how it all comes together.

I recommend that role play be done on a very regular basis, among all members of your team, not just those who handle phone calls. Every interaction in the office needs to be role played frequently so that it does come out naturally, even though it's scripted. Yes, it's scripted. Role players work from a written script, especially at first, so everyone can use the best words for maximum effect every time. Each step in The Ultimate Patient Experience, including the steps covered in this book and a large number of additional steps besides, can and should be role played.

These steps include patient phone calls, greeting patients, patient transfers, patient follow-ups, and patient checkouts. Role play also means that you too get to join in on the fun.

As the dentist in your dream practice, you should role play handovers when you arrive in the treatment room, interactions during the course of treatment, and handovers at the end of treatment. You also need to role play interruptions that require you to leave a patient in the middle of treatment. In particular, you need to know how to handle those interrupting phone calls.

Treatment Interruptions: Practicing Time Outs

Most dental practices don't correctly screen calls that come in for dentists while they are treating patients. It amazes me that some practices don't screen such calls at all. Someone just marches into the treatment room and says, "Dr. Lawson, your wife is on the phone," or "Dr. Lawson, your bank manager is calling for you." And Dr. Lawson says, "Tell them I'll be right with them," puts down his instruments, and leaves the room.

If you've developed any kind of Customer Service Eyes by now, you can see what that does to the patient. The announcement of the phone call itself creates an immediate alarm in the patient's mind, followed shortly by the thought, "Wait, I'm paying for this. Why is this guy leaving me sitting here while he's taking a call?"

You need to have a procedure in place to screen calls and handle truly urgent ones. This can be as simple as having your front office person step in and quietly and discretely show you a note. This allows you to excuse yourself by saying, "Mrs. Smith, let me give you a short break. I'm just going down to do a brief check next door, and I'll be back shortly." You can then go off to take your phone call without your patient feeling inconvenienced at all.

And of course, if you have a procedure in place, you and your front office have to practice it.

Full Team Practice: Weekly Meetings

Dentists who view their weekly staff meetings as nothing more than rundowns on the week are missing a critical opportunity for excellence (not to mention they're probably boring their poor teams to death). When done correctly, weekly meetings are like full scale practices by professional sports teams: they're opportunities to not only get in some practice but also to motivate, assess, and build "spirit" in your team.

To maximize the benefits of your weekly team meeting, everyone's got to be there in body and mind. Timing is important. Never have your meetings first thing in the morning, last thing in the afternoon, or just before lunch. Those are notorious times for causing office schedules to fall behind, so your meeting will either be rushed or rescheduled. Never schedule your meeting as a "working lunch," either. People can't focus properly on the business at hand when they're fiddling with a salad or sandwich. Generally, I find timing weekly meetings just after the lunch hour works best.

Meetings can be both professional and fun. In fact, a bit of fun makes them work even better. You don't want your team to be just sitting there tapping their pencils or gazing out the window, so start with a little bit of role play. You just get two people up there and say, "Right, we're going to role play this handover from Mrs. Taylor who's had three fillings," or "We're going to role play this treatment interruption." It only takes a couple of minutes to do, it provides practice for the role players, and it reinforces procedures for the rest of the team to see. Plus, it breaks the ice of the meeting, since role play on demand doesn't have to be perfect. Role play at weekly meetings is intended as a way to give and get feedback, a fun way to exchange knowledge and get everyone involved.

I think all good offices have a basic agenda for weekly staff meetings that includes a review of numbers and standard business items. For offices that are committed to The Ultimate Patient Experience, a review of the World Class Customer Service processes and procedures that you've put in place should precede standard business on the agenda. Review these processes and procedures with an eye on what worked well during the week and what didn't work so well. And even if you have a fair number of deficiencies to address, celebrate your successes. At my team meetings, I announce these successes. I will say, "Mary did really well with a problem in the treatment room this week," or "Janice really stepped up to the plate when Betty's daughter was sick."

I also encourage adding a brief item to your weekly agenda that allows a few team members to share information on their roles with others. Tap a few team members in advance and ask them to give a report on a little-known aspect of their jobs, something they do that other team members aren't aware they do. It's a terrific way to give every player a chance to shine while educating the rest of the team.

Once you've covered these Customer Service bases, you can move on to the general business items. The entire meeting should take about 45 minutes. And if any goals were achieved—if your office made its daily collection or production quota, for example—you celebrate them with thanks, praise, and reward.

My office team regularly knocks it out of the park, so we usually end meetings with a grab bag. It's just a bag full of bills, and all the team members get to stick their hand in and pick one out. All but one of the bills are the same. They might all be $10.00 bills except for one $20.00 bill or even a bunch of $20.00 bills and one $50.00 bill. If you have a big staff, you may want to put the bills in small envelopes or plastic eggs so everyone can open them all at once. Otherwise, the last person to pick from the bag will know if the big bill has already been pulled out.

I've had clients look at me in disbelief when I bring up the grab bag method, but once they use it, they find out how worthwhile it is. Do the math. If you have a staff of 15 people, that $10.00 grab bag will cost you $160.00, including the $20.00 bill. That's nothing compared to the profits you realize when your team hits their weekly goal, and it's even less compared to the profits you'll realize from the additional goals they'll now start meeting!

You see, as lovely a surprise as that $10.00 is, the money isn't really what's at work here. It's what the money *represents* that is going to bring more money in. If Betty had found $10.00 on the sidewalk this morning, she'd have been tickled, but it wouldn't have powerfully changed her day. What changes the day for people is the feeling they get when you do something for them that shows them that you think that they're special.

The magic that that $10.00 bill works on Betty is the same magic that The Ultimate Patient Experience works on your entire dental practice. It shows others they matter to you as people. And people who feel valued respond in wonderful ways.

The Best Compliment Ever

I love it when a new patient tells me, "Your practice is so warm and friendly. I've never been anywhere like this before." It's nice to get compliments like that. They're confirmation that our practice is meeting its mission to provide Customer Service that's truly World Class. Recently, however, we received a slightly different compliment, and it was the finest we could ever receive.

The compliment came from Dorothy, who'd been coming to see us for years and years. Both she and her husband, Peter, are terrific patients and terrific people. I've seen them regularly for everything from hygiene visits to smile improvements. They were originally referred to me by their daughter-in-law, Alison, whose teeth I straightened prior to her wedding. Actually, the wedding date had to be pushed back because of the braces. We still laugh about that.

Anyway, Peter had a short appointment to see me one Wednesday, and he canceled it on very short notice. He called only a few hours in advance to say something urgent had come up, and he would call

Continued on next page

back later to reschedule. My wife, Jayne, took the call, and she could hear the alarm in his voice. She asked him if he was all right, and all he would tell her is that he had a family issue.

Of course, we were concerned. And when Peter called back a few days later to reschedule, we discovered our concern was well founded. The reason he had had to change his appointment was that his family had suffered an enormous loss. A death had occurred under tragic circumstances. Their son's wife had just been given the news that her full-term baby had died before birth and was going to be stillborn. Sadly, these were circumstances that my wife and I had experienced too. Because of this shared history, Jayne was able to reach out to Dorothy and offer advice as well as truly heartfelt condolences and sympathies.

And it was during one of these moments that Dorothy said to Jayne, "Oh my goodness. I've just realised. You're not our dentist. You're actually our friends."

That's what it's all about. It's about being a friend first, because everyone needs a friend.

The Surefire Sign of Success

Daniel is one of my very first dental coaching clients. We've formed a long-term relationship and have become good friends. That does my heart good, because long-term relationships are the heart of success in life and in business. Just the other day, Daniel himself reminded me of this fact.

When I picked up his call, I thought he was phoning to check in as usual, but he had very special news.

"David, you won't believe who came in to see me! Kathy!"

Now, I'd never met Kathy, but I knew very well who she was. Daniel was an excellent study; he committed to providing The Ultimate Patient Experience in his office, so he tracked his patients carefully. Despite his best efforts, however, he'd lost touch with a patient named Kathy. He'd brought it up a couple of times, since he really liked Kathy, and she seemed to like his practice. She'd even referred quite a few patients to him. Then, after years of regular visits and what seemed to Daniel to be a very strong relationship, Kathy missed an appointment. Calls from the office went unanswered. She was gone.

Of course, Daniel thought about Kathy over the years. He valued and cared about her. So when he learned that she'd only recently called to make an appointment—after three years!—he couldn't wait to see her and make sure she was all right. Thankfully, she was. Life had just gotten away from her, she told him, and since she hadn't had any problems with her teeth, a variety of circumstances had simply kept her from coming in. But then she *did* encounter a dental problem and, as she shared with Daniel, "I told my husband I needed to have this taken care of and no one but Dr. Daniel was going to work on my teeth!"

You can't imagine how thrilled Daniel was or how thrilled I was for him. You see, Kathy now lived three hundred miles away from Dr. Daniel's dental practice. Yet, in her eyes, Daniel was still her dentist. Kathy was living proof of how much Daniel's hard work on delivering great service had mattered. She was a surefire sign of his success.

The Value of a Coach

The professional golfer who practices his swing regularly to keep it in tip-top shape doesn't practice alone. He does so with a coach at his side to give him feedback, keep him focused, and make him better. The longer he works with the right coach, the better he's going to be.

Building the practice of your dreams is the same. You can study up and make some vast improvements, but you're going to get farther faster, with the right coach. Providing The Ultimate Patient Experience to all your patients is a goal, but it's also an ongoing process. Even when you achieve a certain level, it has to be constantly monitored, refined, and improved upon so you can get to the next level. I can't emphasize how tough this can be without a coach. The intricacies of running a dental practice, let alone running it properly from the get-go, are challenging enough for any dentist. Really, all dentists are, and all dentists want to be, is "technicians." We just want to be repairers and fixers of teeth. That's all.

As you know, when you're a dentist, you've always got your back to the office. You've got your head in someone's mouth. You need to rely on things that are, literally, going on behind your back to run like clockwork. Under such conditions, clockwork is far more attainable when you've got someone on constant surveillance for you, helping you and working with you, giving you reminders and input.

That's what my best clients are realizing. They're getting astronomical changes in their figures and the quality of their lives when the right processes are implemented and they've got an extra pair of eyes and an extra brain—mine—watching to make sure that they've implemented these processes correctly and helping them with things they're not really up on yet.

To paraphrase the brilliant entrepreneur Seth Godin, "advice that's simple, guaranteed, and easy isn't worth as much if it's free." He said, "if it was, everyone would be successful. The advice really worth following can be tough to execute on your own, but it's far easier when you pay for it. If it's worth asking for, it's worth having someone show you how to do it and do it right."

Satisfied Patients. Satisfied Clients.

It wouldn't be right for me to devote an entire book to providing World Class Customer Service in *your* business without addressing the World Class Customer Service that I provide to the clients I coach. I asked one of those clients to address what she's gotten out of working with me, and here's what she had to say:

> "I've been running my own dental practice for almost ten years, and I found myself getting frustrated with long work hours, stressful days, and profits that were good but not really great. I knew something had to change, but I didn't know what that something was. So I began looking for a consultant to help me.

I looked at quite a few coaches and chose David for several reasons. He was the only one I found who was actually a dentist, and having someone who truly understood the dentistry side of running a practice was really important to me. I didn't want an outsider who was simply taking a run at my practice using a business approach.

I've been working with David for only six months so far, and I've upped my collections by an average of $40,000.00 monthly. In fact, I recently smashed my new target of $100,000.00 a month by $25,000.00. What's impressive to me is that these changes happened without spending one additional penny on marketing. In fact, I've actually spent less money on marketing while my bottom line has increased. It's all been due to retaining more patients and improving productivity in my practice. Everything is much more organized and sane, and I've also been able to hire additional staff.

David's approach has really opened my eyes to the importance of Customer Service. It's given me the focus to take my business in the direction I want to, as well as the confidence to go there. It's also made my team and me excited to come to work every day. I've learned a lot about myself in the process. I've learned that I'm actually a very good business owner; I've got a good head for business and am quite entrepreneurial; and I'm a great leader of a great team.

When I first told my team I was bringing in a coach, I'll admit I got some mixed reactions. But David's methods quickly got them on board and made them more positive and passionate about the work they do. They're willing to try new things, and watching them grow into their potential has been wonderful. It's taken a huge amount of pressure off me. I now know I don't have to try to do everything myself. My team and I can work together, and together we'll continue to make the practice grow.

The advice I'd give to any dentist who's thinking, "How can I grow my practice?" is definitely get some outside help. A fresh pair of eyes takes you away from the day-to-day grind and allows you to step back and really take a look at what's going on in your dentistry business. Having someone like David to help me identify areas that needed improvement and guide me through the process of making those improvements has been tremendous for me.

I'd recommend David without reservation. Initially, we signed on for a twelve-month relationship, but I can't see that ending anytime soon. Now that I've taken my practice to a new level of success, I'm excited to reach the next level, and I know that David can help me accomplish that."

ABOUT THE AUTHOR

David Moffet is fifty-five years old and has been a dentist for thirty-two years, practicing in the same location in Parramatta, New South Wales, for the last twenty-eight of those years. At the time of writing, he works there three days per week.

David lives in northern Sydney with his wife, Jayne, and their two adult children, for most of the week. He and Jayne also spend part of each week two hours southwest of Sydney on their sixty-eight-acre property, where they raise beef cattle.

David is a keen walker and golfer, though an arthritic right shoulder joint has restricted his golfing of late. He likes to follow and watch the Penrith Panthers Rugby League team. He is also a closet KISS fan but has never painted his face.

Despite David's lean stature, he is a keen foodie and enjoys eating out. He and Jayne also love to travel. Through his coaching, David loves meeting up with clients and friends across Australia, New Zealand, the United States, and the United Kingdom.

When David finally hangs up his hand piece, he and Jayne hope to spend more time at the farm, reading all the books he has collected and hasn't yet read.

HOW TO CONTACT DAVID

The best way to get in touch with David is via e-mail:
david@theUPE.com

or via Facebook:
https://www.facebook.com/davidmoffet

David can also be found on Twitter,
Pinterest, Instagram, and LinkedIn.

You can subscribe to his twice-weekly dental blogs at:
http://www.ultimatepatientexperience.com.

CPSIA information can be obtained
at www.ICGtesting.com
Printed in the USA
BVHW010358130220
572027BV00045B/416/J